# THE YEAR OF THE KOALA

# THE YEAR OF
# THE KOALA

H. D. Williamson

ILLUSTRATED BY

William T. Cooper

CHARLES SCRIBNER'S SONS / NEW YORK

Library of Congress Cataloging in Publication Data

Williamson, Henry Darvall.
  The year of the koala.

  Bibliography: p. 205
  Includes index.
  1. Koalas.  I. Title.
QL737.M38W54          599'.74446          75-12706
ISBN 0-684-14351-8

1 3 5 7 9 11 13 15 17 19 V/C 20 18 16 14 12 10 8 6 4 2

PRINTED IN THE UNITED STATES OF AMERICA

*To my wife*

# CONTENTS

# PREFACE

Although millions of people are familiar with the general appearance of the koala, it is probably safe to say that almost all of them would be prepared to admit that their acquaintance with this interesting little creature is really quite superficial.

By comparison with our knowledge of certain other wild animals that have attracted public attention, we know very little about the koala. The lion and the ape, for instance, and many others have been subjects for the artist, the writer, and the scientist since before the days of ancient Babylon. But, in spite of its widespread popularity, the koala remains something of a mystery—though it does possess at least one characteristic that soon becomes evident and gives the observer some insight into its habits. *Phascolarctos cinereus* is essentially an inactive animal, which implies, correctly, that most of the wanderings of the full-grown koalas in the following story have been forced on them.

This is so because the part of Australia which is the koala's habitat—the eastern coastal area—also happens to be that part of the continent where development is proceeding fastest. And this, in turn, is the main reason why the narrative tells of what happens to one of the small communities which have managed to survive catastrophic changes in the environment and are still existing, precariously, in "islands" of food trees scattered throughout their original range.

Of course there are still koalas living remote from the operations of men in the northern coastal forests of Queensland, and a story about them would also be interesting, even though it could be quickly told. But it would surely be somewhat irrelevant, for the developments taking place in one region today will probably be taking place in other regions tomorrow—reserves and national parks being excepted here for the purposes of the argument.

The preceding books in this series, *The Year of the Whale* and *The Year of the Seal*, both by Victor B. Scheffer, and *The Year of the Butterfly* by George Ordish, have set a standard for uncompromising truth in storytelling, and *The Year of the Koala* is similarly based on fact, the various incidents described having come in the main from observations made in the field. These have been fitted into a mosaic with a nonrecurring pattern to give continuity. Because of the actual transportation of koalas from one place to another by the rangers of the National Parks and Wildlife Service and the evidence of the subsequent movements of the animals as revealed by numbered ear tags, much of this pattern formed itself.

Rod Pearse, a biologist with the Australian National Parks and Wildlife Service of New South Wales, maintains there is a little informed guesswork in the story. Well, maybe there is. But if a koala with a tag of a certain color in its ear and with certain numerals thereon is recorded at site X on June 20, then recorded again three days later at site Y, it is surely not unreasonable to suppose that the animal has made its way unaided from X to Y in a period of three days or less. And if there are a road and a creek running between X and Y, it is similarly not unreasonable to suppose that the koala walked across the road and swam the creek—especially when it is known that koalas are good swimmers and that they will cross a concrete highway as nonchalantly as they would a flat rock in a wilderness.

The story is set in New South Wales because it is the region I know best and is a state where the removal of forests has been carried out on a large scale. However, not all the koalas in New South Wales have been displaced, and conditions there at present can be said to be intermediate between the extremes which exist, or existed until recently, in some of the forests of Queensland in the north and in the most closely settled part of Australia—Victoria, in the south.

*Koala* is an aboriginal word meaning "the animal that never drinks" or, possibly, "the animal that is able to exist without drinking." Actually, koalas have been known to lap water occasionally, though a healthy koala never bothers to go in search of it. The names of the male and female koalas whose fortunes are followed in the narrative, Boorana and Talgara, are also aboriginal—*boorana*, "smoke," and *talgara*, "cloud." Both koalas are gray, the male the darker of the two. Most of the animals from the middle section of the koala's range are gray, or grayish, while those in the north are inclined to be tawny and those in the south, brown or dark gray.

In gathering material for the book, I have had the assistance of a number of people, in particular Rod Pearse, who has already been mentioned and who has been most generous with his time in discussing and demonstrating his work with koalas. Tony Barclay-Rose, also of the N.P.W.S., has supplied many helpful data from his records of the Ku-ring-gai Chase area, while Stuart Heilbron, the wild-life ranger for a tremendous expanse of country of which Lismore is the center, and Oliver McCullough of Wood-burn are others to whom "nothing is a trouble."

Frank Cockram, a microbiologist at the Colin Blumer District Veterinary Laboratory, Armidale, New South Wales, a glimpse of whose work on keratoconjunctivitis in koalas is given in the July chapter, provided information which would not otherwise have been available at the time, as did John McNamara of Koala Park at Pennant Hills, near Sydney, and Russell K. Dickens, the veterinary surgeon who, with John McNamara's assistance, is at present carrying out experiments to discover just how the koala's system deals with the considerable oil content of eucalyptus leaves.

Edward P. Finnie, the head veterinarian at the Taronga Park Zoo in Sydney, where many koalas which have been hit by cars or attacked by dogs, as well as orphaned young ones, are brought for treatment, described some of the cases he has had to deal with and the curative methods used. Thanks are due also to Dave Thomas, the keeper in charge of marsupials at the zoo and a man with a keen and sympathetic eye for those quirks of behavior which so often impart character to an animal, be it a koala or a camel.

Mrs. C. Adams and Raymond W. Patterson, both members of the Avalon Preservation Trust, have given much information on the koalas in their locality, and I never quite became used to hearing over the phone that there was a koala with a cub on her back in the front garden of a house in Newport or Clareville.

Thanks also to Douglas L. Dixon, Harold J. Pollock, Roy Ritchie, and Arthur Wilkinson. Roy Ritchie has been watching koalas in the gray gum trees around his house for thirty years. He says koalas make good neighbors. They are considerate. They do not try to get into the roof spaces of houses to live there—or, worse, die there; they do not eat rosebuds or fruit or vegetables or dig holes in lawns or scratch up garden beds, and except in the mating season they seldom raise their voices. Incidentally, Roy Ritchie thinks that large dogs are a more serious threat to koalas today than are automobiles.

As some words used in the text may be puzzling to readers, a glossary has been added. Also, as the seasons in Australia differ from those in the northern hemisphere, some readers may have to pause occasionally to take a bearing, as in the June chapter, where the first month of winter ends in fine, warm, sunny days and cool, starry nights.

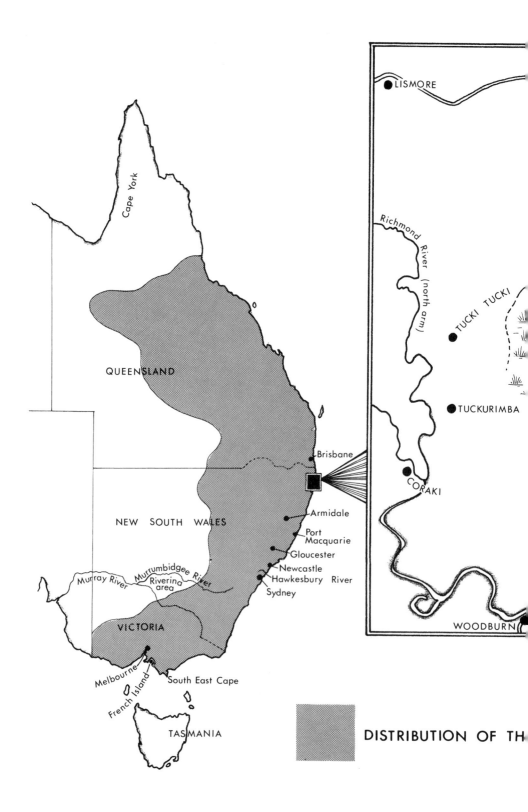

Cape York

QUEENSLAND

NEW SOUTH WALES

Murray River

Murrumbidgee River

Riverina area

VICTORIA

Melbourne

French Island

South East Cape

TASMANIA

Brisbane

Armidale

Port Macquarie

Gloucester

Newcastle

Hawkesbury River

Sydney

LISMORE

Richmond River (north arm)

TUCKI TUCKI

TUCKURIMBA

CORAKI

WOODBURN

DISTRIBUTION OF TH

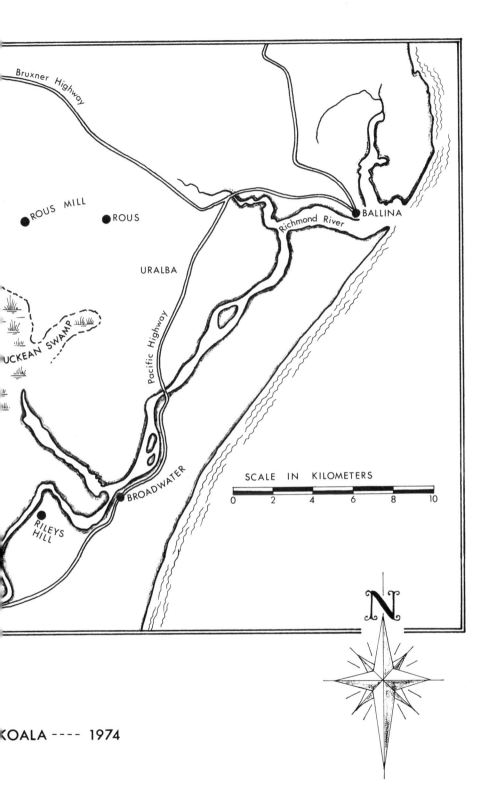

Bruxner Highway

ROUS MILL    ROUS

URALBA

Richmond River

BALLINA

Pacific Highway

UCKEAN SWAMP

BROADWATER

RILEYS
HILL

SCALE   IN   KILOMETERS

0     2     4     6     8     10

N

KOALA ---- 1974

# DECEMBER

The wedge-tailed eagles above the seaward slopes of the Blue Mountains are two black specks circling. Yet the air is so clear that, once sighted, they are easy to keep in view. The temperature has fallen considerably since noon, but this is December, the first month of summer, and the day is still hot.

Seventy, perhaps eighty, kilometers east, the ocean is plainly visible. Westward, the afternoon sun has veined the highlands with a labyrinth of somber straits and narrows, and the shadows are as dark as the light is scintillating, a wind from the parched interior having blown away the coastal humidity. There are no half-tones.

Much of the country spread out beneath the two great birds is in its natural state, especially the more rugged parts, but nearly all that lies between the ranges and the

3

sea has been cleared for farms and pastures. There are townships, too, and roadways winding through the hills and spearing across the flats. On the shoreline, but well to the south, the city of Newcastle sends up its puff of smoke, and much farther away, so faint as to be scarcely discernible even from that height and on such a brilliant day, a smudge on the horizon marks the position of Sydney.

The terrain now directly below the eagles is scored with fissures and rock clefts, its trees and bushes being too sparse to have any softening effect, though a patch of dense foliage does flourish in at least one of the gullies, where eucalypts and turpentines are growing in what must be a fair depth of soil. There are some rain-forest trees, too—the brush boxes—which are sufficiently adaptable to grow in other kinds of habitats also. They are with the turpentines in the middle of the gully.

This pleasant-seeming enclave is about five hundred meters long by about half that in width and is completely cut off on the western side by an escarpment which runs north and south to the limits of sight. The escarpment is spectacular in another way too, for its crest is strewn with boulders, and it is from somewhere among these that two ravens suddenly fly up. Seeing the ravens rise, the eagles come sailing down.

The male alights first and claims the prize, a brush-tailed possum, only to be forced away by his stronger, heavier partner. Setting one foot on the dead animal, she bends her fierce head and strips a piece of flesh from the shoulder, which has already been laid bare by the ravens. She eats no more, however, but launches out from the cliff's edge and, flapping heavily over the gully, shapes course for her eyrie, the possum trailing from her talons.

Dusk is not far away, though the light sparkles like surf on the tops of the restless trees, and the sky, swept clean, is full of sunshine. But the clamorous rainbow lorikeets, swift as flights of arrows, are leaving the blossoms of the eucalypts, and the ravens who were robbed of their find by the eagles have started to work back in the direction of their roosting places in the hills, their black wings seeming to brush the rocks as they beat into the wind.

Behind them the shadow of the escarpment flows across the gully like a tide. It rises around the trunks of the tallow-woods, the blackbutts, and the forest red gums and darkens further the dark green leaves of the turpentines; it closes over the saplings and smaller trees and, in reaching for the higher branches, momentarily underlines, as it were, a grayish ball that is visible one moment and hidden in waving foliage the next.

The koala is so far from the trunk of a towering black-butt that the part of the branch where she is resting is no thicker than a man's wrist, and the vertical offshoot in front of her is even thinner. But her slender support is also resilient, though it sways dizzily, dipping and lifting in the gusts. The koala has been asleep since dawn, except for about half an hour's feeding in the late morning. When she rides into the sunshine her fur is misty gray; when she is doused in shadow she seems to be dark brown. She is curled forward so that the highest part of her is the nape of her neck; her forehead is butted against the upright prong of the fork, and both forepaws are folded across her chest. Her hind paws are folded too and pressed against, but not gripping, the vertical offshoot to prevent her from becoming too tightly wedged into her chosen position. She is resting on the small of her back rather than on her rump and, except for the projection of her rounded ears, is a perfect ovoid. Incredibly, she is not clinging on. She is balanced there.

Of course her fur is thick enough to be grooved by the pressure of her body on both extensions of the fork, and this helps to keep her steady, though her obvious confidence in her own safety probably comes most of all from an amazing sense of balance that can trigger her claws into action almost before there is danger of falling.

At last only the tops of the tallest trees are shining in the sun, and they are shining red. Few of the lorikeets are left, and as they go, silently and without excitement, the koala bestirs herself and reluctantly, for all the world like a human being awakening from an afternoon nap, scratches her ear and yawns. Then she yawns again and peers around in the shortsighted, faintly displeased manner of one regretfully preparing to accept once more the fact that there are other things in life besides rest.

Also, because of the smoothness of her face, which is without well-defined brows or muzzle, the strange little marsupial might be said to give an impression of sleepy, slightly befuddled boredom. Her eyes are brown, round, and relatively small for an animal chiefly nocturnal in habit. Her nose, though black and leathery, is in shape not unlike a broad, rather flat human nose and, seen from the front, scarcely interrupts the smooth curve of her face.

Nor is her characterization of a member of another species yet complete, for, in proceeding further toward a state of activity, she flexes one hind leg and then the other, only turning definitely into a koala again as she spreads wide her great hooked claws to show the first two joined together, they and her two stronger outer talons being oddly different from her nailless great toe. When she has stretched she stands up, her hind feet now grasping the branch, and one front paw, two of its claws opposing the other three, locked powerfully around the vertical offshoot. Her limbs are so stout, her feet so wide, and her talons so sharp and strong that her hold surely must be much more powerful than that of her fellow frequenters of the trees, the possums.

Hunger is the only reason for this period of diurnal activity, in which she negotiates with leisurely expertness the waving, unstable world about her. She leans out to grab at some leaves, but they dance tantalizingly away, so she returns to the main trunk and climbs until she is full thirty meters above ground, when she again moves along one of the laterals. Here, in a green cloud of leaves, she selects those she finds most pleasing to her palate, often rejecting some, however, after sniffing at and even after tasting them. In eating she is as unhurried as in her other actions, generally chewing each leaf separately and showing no disposition to crop the foliage.

When she has plucked the leaves within reach, she walks farther along the lateral, pausing once to sit down, one hind foot locked around her thin perch, while she uses the joined claws of the other to scratch the lower part of her back and to give, in this casual operation, an extraordinary display of the arts of the contortionist and the tight-rope performer. Swaying easily with the swing of the bough, she then shuffles on to a fork very like the one she was occupying lower down.

Although her appetite is not wholly satisfied, the black-butt is not a favorite food tree and, in any case, the time for serious feeding is not yet, so she curls up again with her forehead pressed against a vertical branchlet and the small of her back taking her weight. Her rump, tailless and represented by the lowest section of her body's curve, is not resting on anything but merely bridges the base of the fork supporting her.

Clearly, with such stout, muscular limbs and claws like eagle's talons, she does not need a tail as possums do, but a tail would make her *look* safer, functioning either as a counterweight or as an extra means of obtaining purchase on a branch. To a groundling, her position seems precarious.

As the light fades, the wind abates. It will cease altogether about sundown but still has enough force to travel on over the closely settled coastal lands toward the seaboard; and in that part of its journey it will not pass over any other place so nearly unaltered by the presence of man as is the gully with the big trees along its lower edges. For this fertile patch not only is so small as to be hardly worth the clearing but is seldom visited by people and then only by those whose special interests make it worth their while to slog through the rough country immediately surrounding it—the bushwalker, for instance, and the scientist. Further-

more, the water supply is uncertain, a disadvantage that
has not worried the koalas, who obtain all the moisture
they need from their food.

In most seasons a rivulet trickles over the escarpment
and falls as spray on detritus green with moss, where ferns,
vines, and the trees that grow in damp places crowd one
another in a miniature jungle; but this year its flow has
been reduced to a film of seepage curtaining down the
cliff's face.

The koala in the topmost branches of the blackbutt
sleeps on into the dusk. The diurnal birds have made their
exits for the day, and soon the tawny frogmouths and the
owls will be emerging from their secret places in the trees.
Almost every one of the furred animals in the area is
nocturnal, and a wombat, early abroad, is already moving
about the forest floor. A brush-tailed possum runs head first
down a tree trunk to pick a big moth from the bark. Unlike the koala, he will eat almost anything—insects, fruit,
berries, small birds, nestlings and small mammals, and,
naturally, eucalyptus leaves and blossoms.

Stars are shining from a cloudless sky when the sleeper
again sprouts a leg and again changes shape. It is not a
dark night. Light is shimmering from the loftier contours
of the little forest, and the wind has dropped to a westerly
drift. Some of the branches of the bigger trees intermingle,
and the koala crosses by this means into a tallowwood.
This has been her first change of trees every night since
she began sleeping in the blackbutt.

She does not start to feed at once, seeming to have been
disturbed by a harsh, somewhat guttural outcry from some-

where not far away. High in a forest red gum, fittingly the tallest tree in the vicinity, Boorana, the biggest and strongest male in the area, is proclaiming his right to his territory and calling to any mature female within earshot. Not that there is any response. Of the two females closest to him, one is so old that she is failing, and Talgara, the koala who has just left the blackbutt for a tallowwood, having been impregnated three weeks ago, in mid-November, is due to give birth in another week or ten days.

Boorana calls again, but again there is no answer. It is not easy to guess how many koalas are in the gully, because they are widely scattered, but it is certain there are not many. Of the mature males, one is on the point of being pushed out altogether by the aggressive Boorana, though the others seem able to keep their territories inviolate. But it is seldom that they trespass, especially over Boorana's boundaries, which are the longest in the gully, bordering as they do upon the central part and reaching so far toward the northern end that the male formerly established there is now about to lose his place. Counting koalas of all ages, there cannot be more than thirty. But counting is not easy, as koalas are not strictly gregarious and do not remain close together, seeming to prefer a solitary existence with the paradoxical proviso that they do not completely lose touch with one another.

Besides the koalas living in the gully, it would be safe to say that not another twenty can be found within a range of fifty kilometers. Yet at one time almost any area of similar extent in eastern Australia supported a population of many hundreds. But that was before the clearing of the land and years of concentrated killing for the skin trade had either wiped them out completely or reduced them to the point of extinction in every region they formerly inhabited except some of the coastal forests of northeastern Queensland, where they may still be seen in fair numbers.

The circumstances, then, that have caused a remnant of the vanished hosts to be cut off and surrounded by the spreading tide of white settlement are not by any means rare. Such a fate, in fact, quite often overtakes wild creatures whose habitat has been bypassed for the time being by the clearing contractor. In this case the situation is particularly well defined because of the smallness of the gully and the contrast between its tall trees and the surrounding harshlands.

It is as though the koalas were on an island, both in point of location and in time; and yet their state is better than it would have been if they had actually been marooned, for the natural increase of the little community is continually offset by the loss of most of the young ones, who eventually stray or are frightened away by Boorana and the other mature males. If it were not for this, the food trees in the gully would certainly have been eaten out and killed by defoliation. As might be expected, the limits placed upon the freedom of the animals by the special conditions in which they are living do necessitate the rigid application of certain behavioral laws which would lose much of their force if the koalas, especially the younger ones, had more room to maneuver. And the days when that might have been possible have long gone.

This lack of space makes it easy for Boorana to keep on

harassing the rather timid rival he has already pushed to the northern tip of the gully, and it is the same lack of space that enables him and the other males to warn off any raiders—though raiders are rare visitors—who may come with hopes of attracting a female or two in order to set up for themselves. There are six mature males living in the gully, and, although none of them has a large territory, all their territories combined occupy the whole of the available area. So the established males are ideally situated: first, because their breeding females tend to remain within the limits of the gully; second, because they are able to frustrate by menaces and, if need be, by force any poaching by outside males; and, third, because they are able to drive out by intimidation or, again if necessary, by physical attack those prospective dangers to their security, their own maturing sons.

Therefore, as long as Boorana and the rest of the full-grown koalas remain firmly where they are, their future seems secure, barring a disaster. Food trees are plentiful, and there is little likelihood that clearing operations will take place on such an isolated speck of land. But the situation is vastly different for the younger animals, whose eventual fate is to wander into the wilderness—and to them the cultivated country farther out is as much a wilderness as are the harshlands immediately encircling the gully.

As for Talgara, she is content to sleep away the days in her blackbutt and occasionally to eat sparingly of its leaves while waiting for darkness before changing to forest red gum, tallowwood, or gray gum. She is a prodigious eater and puts away more than half a kilogram of food every twenty-four hours. Indeed, the need to eat a lot and often may be the main reason she is semi-nocturnal instead of wholly nocturnal. Fifteen or so hours of summer daylight would be too long to spend in fasting when so much bulk is required. Koalas, however, are very efficient eating machines, and, in order to cope with their massive and specialized intake of eucalyptus leaves, their digestive systems are equipped with a supplementary tract and storage space in the shape of a caecum, or blind tube, of generous diameter and of a length more than four times that of their bodies. The precise nature of this organ and its workings are yet to be investigated.

It was once thought that the oils in eucalyptus foliage were one of the basic food requirements of the koala and that they had a considerable influence on the animal's selection of leaves. It is now suspected, in the light of recent experiments—which admittedly are not yet complete—that the koala may reject all or nearly all these oils.

By the beginning of the second week in December, at least one of the eucalypts close to the blackbutt—the gray gum especially favored by Talgara—is showing signs of raggedness as a result of her continual browsing. During this period of her life Talgara seldom moves far from the trees she has chosen for her daytime quarters and rarely gives any impression of being aware of the different kinds of creatures that live in the gully or visit it, unless they chance to pass very close to her.

Almost every night a series of whirring cries becomes quickly louder as a pair of gliding possums makes volplane after volplane from the southern end of the gully, often to alight finally on the base of a tree near her, the soft but distinct thuds of their landings immediately followed by a rattling of bark as the big gliders claw their way up the trunk. But once among the gum blossoms of the topmost branches, they move as surely and as easily as the tiny pygmy possums. They are so quiet that at times it seems they must have launched out unseen on another journey; then the silence is broken by a sudden swish of leaves, and a dark shape swings from one plume of foliage to another. There, in an atmosphere redolent of honey, they may stay for an hour or so before planing back in the direction from which they came, long tails flying out straight in the airstream. Talgara seldom notices. She is vulnerable only when on the ground, and so the movements of animals in trees are of no importance. On one occasion when the call of a powerful owl—a bird so large that it is sometimes called an eagle owl—terrified the gliders into immobility, Talgara was walking along a branch, a perfect mark for the bird of prey. But she seemed not to hear. Unlike the gliders, she is too heavy for the largest of these powerful owls to carry off.

It is another week or so before the female koala, after staring long and fixedly into the moonlit forest land about her, backs down to the junction of a wide branch and the trunk of a forest red gum and sits there with her front paws by her sides, waiting. Her position is different from the one she usually adopts when sleeping. She is not so hunched up, and her neck is only slightly bent. Since it is impossible for a human being even to know exactly what any other human being, let alone a koala, is seeing, hearing, or feeling, the kind of signals received by Talgara when the birth of her young one is imminent must remain a mystery, but it does seem that she is partly insensible. Certainly she does not notice the tiny sugar glider that alights just above her head and runs quickly toward the higher branches.

Talgara keeps very still. Then she moves slightly, and a jet of reddish fluid springs from between her hind legs and stops. It is some minutes before the new living thing appears.

It is almost as long as the first joint of a woman's little finger and bears no more resemblance to its mother than it does to any other formed creature. It is pinkish, hairless, semi-transparent, and streaked with scarlet blood vessels. It is glistening wet and it has arms, or forelegs, which are small enough in themselves but disproportionately large when compared with the rudimentary hind legs so tightly pressed against its sides that they are discernible only in the same way as the shape of an insect is discernible beneath the shining semi-transparent skin of its chrysalis. Amazingly, it climbs. Its tiny forelimbs are furnished with microscopic, needle-fine claws, and the limbs move, reaching forward and up, clambering, hauling the rest of it higher through the dense, soft fur of the koala's belly. The blind, masked head rolls from side to side with the effort of each stroke. By comparison with the body, the head is large, and long rather than broad. The ears as well as the eyes are sealed, and there are three holes in the squarish muzzle, one being the mouth and the other two, nostrils.

It seems fitting that the sense of smell, which is so highly developed in koalas, should be already operative. A silvery trail, fine as a thread, keeps glinting and vanishing in the moonlight as the tree shadows sway.

Sometimes the living creature pauses. Then it moves on again, blindly yet purposefully, though not with absolute certainty, for the trail is veering, so much so that it soon becomes clear that the opening to the pouch will be missed.

The tiny voyager is lost. It stops, stranded half a hand's-breadth wide of the entrance to the pouch and slightly above it. Talgara does not move. She makes no effort to assist and shows neither concern nor even awareness.

The opening to a koala's pouch is relatively much closer to the cloaca than is the case with kangaroos and wallabies, and a deviation made in the first seconds in the life of a minute-old koala can quickly result in just such a situation as has already developed. The mistake having been made, the traveler must now descend.

Suddenly the "embryo" moves again, and the amorphous body with the swollen arms and the eyeless protuberance that may one day become a head resumes its laboring overarm progress. Stroke by painful stroke, it turns, then slowly makes its way horizontally across the soft belly fur and, inclining downward, reaches the entrance to the pouch and disappears. Once inside, the questing mouth finds one of two teats there and immediately attaches itself, the swelling end of the teat and the contracting muscles of the "gum-baby's" mouth forming a connection strong enough to support the present weight of the young one and also its increasing weight over the next few months. Otherwise the suckling, its flare of energy burned out, would fall off and die.

Because Talgara bred last season and has only recently parted company with her cub, there is actually only one teat for the "embryo" to claim in this instance; the teat used by her previous offspring is too enlarged to be encompassed by the newcomer's tiny mouth.

In the years before protective laws, when koalas were shot in large numbers, many an inquiring hunter, on pulling a young one from the teat of a freshly killed animal, would tear away the tissues of its mouth. The bleeding that then occurred, together with the embryonic appearance and miraculous smallness of the newborn koala, led to the belief that it grew on the teat like a bud—a theory that persisted for years in spite of scientific assurances that an event of this kind was an impossibility.

Birth, migration, and attachment being complete, it might be thought that Talgara would show some sign of preparing to move, but instead she remains immobile for another quarter of an hour. When she does come to life again, she climbs to a considerable height. There is little breeze, and the sounds of the night are distinct in the quiet; the scent of honey from nearby gum blossoms is strong but has no attraction for the koala. Nevertheless, she does hold up her head alertly for a while to smell, to sift, to distinguish, and to savor—almost to weigh, if that were possible—the many odors adrift on the night air; and it is then that an observer may feel he is watching a level of performance possible only because the koala's olfactory organs occupy a far greater proportion of the skull than is the case with most other animals.

Talgara starts to eat again. She has a certain amount of leeway to make up. She hears the crackling of dead sticks in the grass as some wallabies come down from the ridges to the sweeter feed of the gully, and she hears the black swans pass high over head, their soft calls fading. Beneath her the bright, moonlit depths of the forest are like an underwater world, she resting on a submarine growth that stretches up toward the surface.

Although Talgara is alone to the extent that no other member of the colony is very close to her, there is no doubt that she would have moved farther away except for the definitive natural boundaries of the gully.

At all events, this lack of apartness evidently causes her no concern, and when the sun rises she has returned to her blackbutt tree and is asleep far out on a horizontal branch. The weather stays fine. Day after day there is no change. When the westerly blows, the light is like diamonds. By the end of December many of the eucalypts are flowering so profusely that their tops are afoam with blossom. It has been another mild, dry month, with a hint of danger from bush fires underlying its pleasantness, a hint that will become a threat by midsummer unless there is rain.

# JANUARY

Good summer weather continues well into January. Sometimes it is blustery, sometimes subdued, and though the wind may shift a few points to the north or to the south, it always blows from inland, from the interior, rising in the morning and dying away in the late afternoon. As the last pink glow of sunset gives place to darkness and the stars, the scribbly gums fringing the escarpment become a black frieze painted on the sky, and the air is so still from then until dawn that the far-off quarreling of possums and the calling of the little boobook owls are distinct even to human ears, as are the occasional cries of Boorana.

This extreme audibility makes it evident that the gully, probably because of its richness as well as its isolation, has attracted a large number of animals. The koalas are the most vocal. It is now the height of their breeding season, and their guttural roarings and mewings and other strange cries sometimes include a variation like a staccato, cut-off human sneeze, and, more rarely, a loud ticking sound uttered four or five times at intervals of a second or so. The mature males make most noise, but there are only five of them left now that Boorana's threats have scared away the rival who had been clinging desperately to a position at the very edge of his territory. What will happen to him as he wanders off into a world of rocky scrub bounded by kinder but fully settled country is quite unpredictable.

Boorana is at his most aggressive during the breeding season, and at his most active. In appearance and general behavior he is far removed from the smaller koalas— usually females—seen on display in zoos and other places, where there may or may not be a faint perfume of eucalyptus from the bundles of foliage supplied by their captors. When he is moving with the wind, a rank and musty odor precedes him, and when he moves against it, he leaves an aerial trail that is a warning to any other male in the vicinity to keep his distance and is a stimulant to females who have not yet felt the urge to mate. He is bulky, powerful, and decidedly ponderous. The discharge from a gland on his chest, which is becoming more copious as Boorana ages, has this year curled a patch of fur into spiky-looking roughnesses and turned it a deep yellowish-brown. He is belligerent, noisy, and suspicious and spends much of his time, when he is not sleeping, in warning off other males. But he shows not the slightest interest in any female, even if she chances to be in his territory, unless the scent of her tells him she is eligible for mating, when he immediately calls to her and seeks her out. He ignores cubs of both sexes. Fully mature male koalas, and those approaching maturity, he menaces whenever they come near him, and if they are so bold as to keep on advancing, he attacks. It is seldom he is challenged. No doubt his food trees smell of the oily exudation from his chest, and this must act as yet another deterrent. He is always back in his favorite forest red gum well before daylight.

Talgara spends most of her days on the dividing line between two territories, one of them Boorana's, as that is where the blackbutt in which she generally sleeps is situated. Since mating in November, she has not ventured far in any direction and, now that her pouch contains a suckling, seems more than ever determined to stay by herself. Not that any other koala ever troubles her, however—with the single exception of the oldest of the females, whom Talgara now hears approaching through the crackling debris on the ground. She herself has just returned to her sleeping place after feeding for most of the night in the gray gum. It is very early in the morning, before any hint of daylight. Claws rasp on the blackbutt's base, and the sounds grow quiet as the intruder gains the smooth bark higher up. Leaning out to the full length of her forelimb, as sailors once leaned from the rigging, Talgara watches the dark form rising steadily through the shadownets cast by the moon, and grumbles warningly. The other stops. They stare at each other; then the old koala resumes her ascent. Shortly before reaching the intent Talgara, she moves along a lateral, stretches up, and swings with the

ease of a gibbon into the one above. From there she jumps
to an offshoot in the same plane and, having negotiated
several more laterals in a similar unimpeded manner, re-
joins the main trunk, the detour having been made so
effortlessly that either she has come that way before or
the ramifications of a forest are to a koala plainly marked
highways, byways, and shortcuts. After climbing a little
farther, she settles herself near a mass of pendent foliage.

She is a gaunt, rangy creature, so skimpily covered that
her ears are practically hairless. Her frontal fur, formerly
white, has been darkened from years of brushing against
tree trunks, and she shows the signs of age, too, in the
urine stains around her rump and in the gray patches on
her lower back. She moves along the branch and, when
nearly in line with the moon, stretches up for some leaves.
But they are not easy to get, and while she remains in
silhouette her emaciated limbs are like charcoal sticks
trimmed with a silvery fuzz of fur. She is in absolute contrast with Talgara, who is so densely furred as to be almost
fluffy, a quality that gives her an apparent roundness of
form she does not really possess. Her ears are heavily
tufted, and the white markings below her jowls look like
the wings of a collar specially designed to keep her white
front in place.

Apparently the mild hostility that initially existed between the two female koalas has already faded, for neither
has uttered a sound for some time. A breeze drifts through
the forest, and the myriad leaves shimmering in the moon's
glare set up a sighing, rustling sound that dies away in
the distance down the gully. Thrusting her nose into a

cloud of foliage, Talgara forgets the presence of a stranger. She seems to be more unnoticing than ever. The "embryo" enclosed within the warm darkness of her pouch is in almost the same state as when it was born about two weeks ago. It—or rather, he—is as blind, as hairless, as pallid, and as tiny. He is small beyond belief. His front limbs, or arms, are still grotesquely out of proportion, but he is fastened securely to a teat which has swelled to such an extent that his mouth would be torn away if he were suddenly pulled free.

He is lying across his parent's body and above the pouch opening, with his mouth attached to the teat on the left side. He is so small that no change is perceptible in the exterior contour of the pouch. But as he grows, the pouch obviously must distend to accommodate him, and it can do this only above its opening. During this process, the opening will be seen more and more plainly to be at the rearward end, opposite to its position in the kangaroos and wallabies. At the present stage of development, however, the suckling is of so ridiculous a size that to Talgara he may well be only an instinct to keep quiet. She wants to be left alone.

But peace in that place proves to be short-lived, and on the following morning—again, well before dawn—Boorana arrives in pursuit of the newcomer, who has not moved out of the blackbutt since she arrived there twenty-four hours ago. However, the grizzled old female, like the younger koala below her, by no means craves company. She mated early last year and, having rejected her offspring a full month ago, should be ready to mate again. But she is nearly nine years old, a great age for a koala living in the wilds, and is failing rapidly. It is hardly likely, then, that her response to the trumpet call of the breeding season will conform with the pattern of the past.

Nor would Boorana go near her at all except that he has been so thoroughly roused by earlier experiences of this night that his own perceptions have been temporarily blunted. Ever since the onset of darkness his growling cries have resounded through the gully, first in loud threatening to a half-grown male whose challenges he has accepted, though they are as yet only implicit in the youngster's behavior, and later in more urgent uproar as he gave chase to one of the females. He was signally unsuccessful in both affairs. The young male eluded him by leaping into the next tree, and, though Boorana could have matched this feat if he had had a firm base for take-off, the branch used as a springboard by the fugitive was so flexible that it proved an insuperable obstacle to the big koala, who is about two and a half times heavier than his son. And the female he approached an hour or so afterward defeated him in somewhat similar fashion—by continuing to retreat along a willowy limb until she reached a point where the danger that the pair of them would crash to their deaths became so great that the frustrated suitor was obliged to turn back.

Talgara, who has returned early to her sleeping place, utters a shrill warning as Boorana, truly enraged, swarms up the massive trunk toward her. But of course he charges past, making at his best speed for the old female koala and another defeat. She does make some attempt to avoid an encounter but, because of her dimmed senses, is so late in taking alarm that her way of escape has been cut off before she really starts to move—and this in spite of the fact that Boorana is certainly not troubling himself to be quiet.

On the contrary, his approach is blustering, confident, and determined. His grunting cries have taken on a curious resonance, as though uttered in a cavern, and apparently he is not aware of anything unusual about the desperate, cornered creature waiting for him—nothing unusual, that is, until he finds himself confronted by an aged spitfire who, in what may well be her last display of fury, is all hostility and wide-spreading talons.

Thunderstruck, Boorana slides backward down the main shaft of the blackbutt, strikes the next lateral, and sits there until the skinny muscularity of the other settles into more rounded form, when he extends his neck in a manner at once inquiring and conciliatory, and sniffs the air. Immediately recognizing the sexless quality of her anger, he again grips the tree trunk and descends—without comment, as it were. The subject is closed. As he passes Talgara on the way down, she moves away, but he does not pause. She hears him slithering down the bark and a thud as he jumps to the ground.

After springing onto the base of his forest red gum, he hangs there awhile, as though on the point of making yet another quest, but it is nearly dawn, so he continues to climb, using both forelimbs together, then both hind limbs. Catching sight of a young male koala in the next tree, he utters, in passing, another in his repertoire of threats. He has only two attitudes toward young koalas, absolute disregard and implacable rancor. The implacable rancor is for any male cub nearing maturity, and the absolute disregard is for all other younglings of either sex.

In general, young female koalas suffer more at the outset than do young males, for most young females seem to be seized with a wanderlust immediately they part company with their mothers. Young males, on the other hand, may spend as long as two years in and around the community after they leave their mothers and are rarely under stress during this time. It is not until they become mature that the picture changes and they suddenly find themselves resented by the holders of territory everywhere. Even in extensive bushland where territories are ill-defined or practically nonexistent, they are intimidated and sometimes attacked by older males. In circumscribed areas where all the land is held, they are inevitably forced right out of the locality by the possessors of the available territory and so have no choice but to retreat into a less suitable environment. If a male should be successful in finding a female in such inhospitable surroundings, he must then, if he is to have any peace, seize his own plot of ground, either by defeating the present holder or by discovering an unclaimed space with food trees.

This task was difficult enough when koalas were plentiful and their habitat unspoiled, for even in those conditions there were always bachelor koalas living out their lives alone. In present conditions, in districts where the timbered country has been cleared, these outcasts are often

hard put to find enough to eat. So the state of a male in
a situation where the good land has been cleared and the
uncleared land is mostly semi-desert is worse than that of
a female. She, if she remains in the locality where she was
born, will certainly mate in due course with one of the
holders of territory there, or, if she has strayed into un-
known country, she will always be accepted into any colony
she may find tucked away in some hidden fastness of the
bush. He may have to spend his life a wanderer in a vast
nothingness.

The stable part of the community in the gully, then,
consists of Boorana and the other holders of territory, together with the mature females, the youngest of whom is
Talgara, whose age is now four years and four months.

It is noon on a hot day at the end of the first week in
January, and Talgara is asleep in the high branches of a
eucalypt. Perched even higher, almost at the very top of
the tree, the oldest of the female koalas is also asleep. She
sleeps more, much more, than she used to and when she
wakes often remains inactive, not even feeding. She is no
longer attractive to look at.

In the middle part of the gully, in a turpentine tree,
another female, a half-sister to Talgara, is resisting the
efforts of her offspring of nearly eleven months to re-establish herself on her back. The affair soon develops into a
struggle, with the young one refusing to keep her distance
and the parent finally retreating to a position where she
cannot be taken by surprise. And there the matter rests,
the cub whimpering and sometimes squealing out at the

top of her voice at her mother now comfortably settled into a fork of a lofty, slim branch. Though they are apart for the time being, it is pretty clear that a final separation has not yet taken place.

There are only two other grown females within hearing range of Boorana at present, and neither of these is ready to mate. One of them, whose fur has been stained red by the bloodwood tree, is in the same state as the half-sister to Talgara in that she has not yet managed to refuse the demands of a cub who is fully weaned and nearly a year old, while the other—the easiest koala in the gully to iden-tify because of the dangling remains of an ear that was ripped by a fox when she was a cub—is without young of any age, her "embryonic" daughter of two months ago having lost her way on the journey to the pouch. Though free to mate again, she shows no signs yet of so doing. With the exception of the aged female who is spending so much of her time in Talgara's "sleeping-tree," the other females have already mated.

It is toward this situation a few nights later that a young adult koala, a bachelor and a stranger in a strange land, comes over the last of the steep, rocky ridges on the east-ern side of the gully. He is one of a number captured by rangers in the northeast corner of New South Wales shortly before an expanse of bush was cleared for housing. All the animals taken were later released in wildlife reserves in various parts of the state, but the koala now approach-ing the gully has strayed away from the habitat selected for him. He is slightly smaller than most of his kinsmen thereabouts—the first-discovered ash grays of the central coast of New South Wales—and of a tawny color. The difference would have been even more marked if he had been consigned to the colder regions of southern Victoria, where the koalas are biggest of all, though their fur is usually dark gray, sometimes brownish.

It is evident that the challenger has not fared well. He never was a good example of the species and is showing the effects of a scarcity of food. Furthermore, his coat is unkempt, a sure sign of ill health in an animal. In his wanderings westward from the coast he has crossed other ridges like the one he is now on, ridges studded with the same twisted eucalypts whose pale branches float in the moonlight and seem to bear no leaves whatever, with only the banksias and the eriostemon bushes dense enough to cast shadows among the rocks.

But with the breeze bringing scents of a kinder place, he goes eagerly down the slope, pausing occasionally to lift his head to test the air. Detecting the various signature odors of other koalas, he shows some excitement and turns abruptly aside to climb the nearest tree. It is an angophora and, crouching along a massive branch, he extends his neck and head so that they make a straight line and then, his open mouth pointing slightly upward, he calls and calls again, his roarings rising and falling with the pumping of his flanks and the expulsion and intake of his breath. His posture has much in common with that of a bellowing bull, and the sound is not unlike a bull's, either, allowing for the relative sizes of the two animals—although the bull which, pound for pound, could match the raider in output of noise would shake the very earth.

When at length an answer comes, however, it is not from any of the females but from Boorana, so the intruder goes no nearer, though he keeps on sending out loud cries at intervals until morning.

Carried on sporadically between dusk and dawn, the vocal contest continues for three nights as the stranger, not daring to make more than an occasional quick sally into hostile territory, hovers uneasily about the fringes of the gully, for this is not a direct attack but only an attempt by a young male to entice away a female for himself. Unluckily for him, no female is interested.

The raider is eventually put to flight when he is surprised by another male and, in his panic, climbs into the tree where Boorana is dozing. But there is no struggle, no physical contest. As always during the hours of darkness, the big koala wakes quickly. He is so bulky and formidable, and his voice so exactly matches his appearance, that the other jumps to a lower branch and then, from a considerable height, to the ground—a feat Boorana dares not attempt. As it is, the fugitive is dazed by the impact and it is some seconds before his wild stumblings turn into the purposeful gallop that carries him up the slope and out of sight. Boorana starts in pursuit but gives up after a few steps.

The moon is at its zenith when the sun rises, and Boorana, worn out by three nights of threatenings and posturings rounded off by a chase that never really got under way and a battle that was never really joined, has been asleep for hours. Victory to him comes as a matter of course; defeat for the loser comes as a disaster, and he will travel far indeed before his calls are heard by any except possums and owls and gliders in ghostly flight between the trees.

If he had been hardy enough to stay in the neighborhood, he might possibly have met with success, as less than a week after his retreat the female with the slashed ear suddenly comes in heat. She is, by chance, not far from the forest red gum where Boorana is usually to be found, and as soon as the big male catches the scent of her he starts to call, and keeps on calling, sometimes in loud, harsh tones, sometimes with strange crooning or rumbling sounds. Claws rasp on the tree's trunk as he slides down to meet his visitor, who is now climbing toward him, and the din of their voices rises to a loud, confused caterwauling.

For a moment the two are side by side; then, as he tries to seize her by the shoulders, the courtship takes on the appearance of a fight until she breaks away and races for the treetops, closely followed by Boorana, whose roarings and guttural cries, unmusical to human ears but no doubt pleasing to a female koala, increase in volume and urgency.

The chase is a boisterous affair, remarkable mainly for its revelation of the strength of the two animals and their climbing ability, especially in direct ascent; but it does seem likely now that, in spite of Boorana's efforts, it will end in much the same way as the other approaches made by him in the last few nights have ended. And this might well have been the case, except that on this occasion the pursued does not seek to escape by retreating along some slim and yielding branch. But even when Boorana does at last overtake her, the action is no less turbulent, she striking at him repeatedly and he crowding her ever more fiercely until copulation takes place in the standard manner of quadrupeds the world over. In slightly over a month—say, thirty-five days—another blob of living matter will set out on its miraculous journey from genital opening to pouch, there to remain until its naked shapelessness has been changed into a miniature of the creature it will one day be.

Right up to and past midsummer many of the eucalypts are bright with blossom—though this may be scarcely worth the mentioning in a land where the seasons often become mixed up with one another and where the climate generally is so equable that some trees flower the year round.

One night near the end of January the gully is the center of a sudden storm, which splits the darkness every now and then with lightning flashes that lay bare a gigantic canvas of violence and of movement, of bent and stream-ing trees and rain-lashed ridges, all painted there, quite still. And always, before the eye can focus properly, the picture vanishes.

In the morning, when the sun rises, Talgara does not appear to be wet, and certainly she is not bedraggled. The day is fine with a soft northeast breeze. Earthy scents, bushland scents of eucalyptus and of honey distill into the cool air. The small forest—small in extent, not in height—in the confined space of the gully is the greener already, its foliage washed. Broken branches are lying on the ground, but their leaves too are bright, for the sun has not yet reached them.

The oldest female in Boorana's territory is in the place she has claimed for her own, near the top of the blackbutt tree. Her fur is drenched. But she is firmly curled into a fork, and soon the sun will be hot enough to dry her.

Talgara wakes about noon and crosses to the other side of the blackbutt. None of the koalas was very active during the night, though, with their skill and strength, they could have moved about if the situation had called for it. After feeding for half an hour, Talgara goes to sleep until the sun is below the escarpment, when she again awakes and repeats the process. But the older koala does not stir.

Soon after dark, Talgara quits the tree where she has had her diurnal sleeping place for some weeks and where also she fed briefly in the daytime when the pangs of hunger awakened her. She establishes herself in a gray gum. It may be that the blackbutt has been denuded of its more succulent leaves, or perhaps its chemistry has undergone a change, as sometimes happens. In any case, it was never a favorite food tree, and she does not return to it in the few months she has yet to live in the gully.

Dawn on the second morning after the storm shows the sole remaining occupant of the blackbutt to be in the same position as she was twenty-four hours earlier. Age and rain driven by the wind have defeated her at last, and death is not far away. Most probably its final cause will be pneumonia, and when koalas die in this manner they die so quietly that there is no way of knowing exactly when life ends. It is not until late afternoon that the curled-up form in the high branches tilts slightly and does not recover, then tilts again, rolls slowly from its place, and plunges to the ground.

# FEBRUARY

Early in February the female koala whose chest fur has been stained by the bloodwood tree approaches Boorana in answer to his calling and, in spite of her failure to rid herself entirely of the company of her well-grown cub, mates with him.

There is now only one other unmated female koala in that part of the gully, Talgara's half-sister—and she too is plagued by an overpossessive young one. However, she is gradually becoming more and more indifferent to the claims of her offspring.

Though she often answers Boorana's cries in her high-pitched voice and generally seems to prefer him to the holder of an adjoining territory, she makes no definite move in his direction. Then the spell of temperate summer weather comes to an end, and, in common with most animals in the district, the koalas lapse into a state of somnolent inactivity.

Within an hour of the change, a heat haze is again shimmering on the rocks of the escarpment. A puff of dust balloons up and floats, dissipating, over the gully as the wind continues from the west.

Always greatly affected by very hot weather, the koalas remain throughout the day and for part of the night sprawled out in the trees in any kind of position that affords relief. Often one looks like a dead body that has fallen from a greater height and been caught in the branches, so grotesque is its attitude—perhaps completely spread-eagled, with its claws seemingly entangled in twigs on either side and its head hanging over the branch where it is lying on chest and belly. When the koalas wake they usually stay in the same place.

In such weather there are very few sounds to be heard in the bush except the skirring of insects. The lorikeets have moved on toward the coast, and though there are many birds in the gully—currawongs, kookaburras, noisy miners, and the smaller honeyeaters—most of these fall silent before midmorning and do not come to life again until the shadow of the escarpment is darkening the trunks of the trees at the bottom of the slope and there is a hint of coolness in the air.

During the heat wave no other creature is as active or as vocal as the currawongs. Sometimes the kookaburras laugh at dawn and in the evenings on the edge of darkness, but more often they fail altogether to send out their clamorous signal, so it is not unusual for the wild, haunting

cries of the currawongs to be the first and last sounds of
the day.

Certainly these big black-plumaged birds liberally slashed
with white are always earliest abroad, flying up in parties
of five or six to swoop and turn and drift against the sky,
calling in their loud, strange voices and then diving into
the trees as into a dark sea. They are on the move all day,
except in the sweltering hush of noon, running about the
branches while their bold golden eyes search out food,
whether it be insects, berries or small birds and nestlings.
They are the swashbucklers of the avian world, not over-
brave but quick to strike when the advantage lies with
them; and they are seldom silent, their repertoire ranging
from a low, lilting whistle to the raucous yells of mob
attack.

When dusk is turning into dark, they are still planing
between the tree trunks on wide recurved wings, or running
over the ground, prying, pecking, equally ready for flight
or fight, timid and fearful one moment and aggressive the
next, as they work their way along the gully, their eerie
hollow-sounding calls becoming gradually fainter.

If the currawongs are the most active of creatures in the
present conditions, the koalas remain the most inactive.
Talgara has moved from the gray gum she selected after
quitting the blackbutt and has climbed into a turpentine,
a tree with dense foliage; and Boorana too has found himself a patch of solid shade low down in his forest red gum,
where the westerly wind, after its journey over the rocky
ridges behind the escarpment, is tempered by the shadows
of many branches. Lassitude, however, does not greatly

impair their appetites. The amount of food required by koalas to provide them with adequate nourishment and also to ensure the proper working of their digestive systems means they rarely go for long without eating, provided there is suitable food available—though of course almost all their feeding is done between dusk and dawn, and very little during daylight hours. But few wild animals adhere hard-and-fast to any rule, and every now and then some koalas will return each morning to sleep in non-food trees, thus forgoing for the period their habit of browsing occasionally by day. Such animals are often early abroad and may sometimes be seen before it is quite dark, making their way toward a favorite eucalypt.

The temperature has remained high for days and is starting to rise further, so it is not surprising that the approaches of any large cub to its parent should be determinedly rebuffed, and this is what has happened between the mother and daughter sheltering in a brush box tree. But the disturbance has ceased for the time being, and there is quiet.

Although the brush box, like the turpentine, does provide a cavern of shade, it is not a preferred food tree, and for this reason, and because of sheer fatigue, neither koala has eaten much since the night before. It is now past noon, and the two seem to be dozing. Flecks of sunlight sway and drift across their fur. The heat presses down. There is no sound in the gully except the murmur of the wind in the treetops until a cicada suddenly creaks into song— and when ten thousand more make it a chorus, the din takes on something of the quality of silence. Shuffling along the branch with unexpected quickness, the young koala makes a last bid for her old place on her parent's back. But that phase of life is past and gone. Furthermore, the grown koala has been so roughly awakened that her reaction is one of uncharacteristic violence, the flash of her reddish front as she stands up to thrust away her offspring of the previous season encouraging the fancy that she may have turned momentarily into another, fiercer animal. As it is, the cub is so surprised that she saves herself from falling only by a split-second grab, which leaves her dangling by the claws of a front foot. But the grip is a good one—the grip of a koala always is—and she has no trouble in doubling the safety factor by clamping a second set of claws beside the first, whereupon she swings "hand-over-hand" along the branch, wailing as though in the last extremity of pain. When her outcries have ceased, she hauls herself up and leaps to the next higher limb. Her dam lazily combs the fur of her side with the joined claws of a hind foot, then slows, stops, folds her paws, bends her head, and adopts the attitude of sleep. The cub does the same. When she awakens after sundown she may eat some of the brush box but more probably will leave it for a gray gum or a forest red gum, there to feed throughout the night. Later she will return to the tree her parent is resting in and may take up a position quite close to her, on the same branch or one nearby. So the process of separation will continue until it is complete.

Most of the koalas living in the gully have been born there, the only exceptions being Talgara and her half-sister, who have come from over in the ranges, where as cubs and adolescents they roamed a vast original forest inhabited by a large, though widely dispersed, koala population.

Because they chanced to cross some cleared ground to a clump of eucalypts left by the bulldozers as shade trees for stock, the two escaped the wildfire which turned most of that region to desolation, and from there they kept on drifting east in a desultory fashion, to reach the same gully within a few weeks of each other. They were immediately accepted by males already established in territories there, and both produced young that year and the year following.

In the present season, the heat wave having ended, the koalas in the gully again bestir themselves at intervals during the day and at night resume their habit of moving from tree to tree in search of the best leaves.

About this time Boorana mates with the half-sister to Talgara, after a boisterous courtship which so terrifies the cub that she backs down the tree trunk, farther away from her mother than she has ever been before; and from that day the distance between the two increases until the young one is living a solitary life with only the slightest association with the other members of the community.

Nor does the process end there; soon both the young female koalas so recently parted from their mothers are wandering farther afield. One strays northward and vanishes into the surrounding wilderness of harshlands and cleared country; the other, after scrambling over the ridge to the east, starts to cross the same kind of broken terrain of rocks and sharp-leaved bushes, gradually working her way closer to the outlying farming areas.

She is a really beautiful little creature, the overfur—

those longish hairs which project beyond the true fur—
darkish on Boorana and on Talgara's half-sister, being in
her case much lighter in color, giving her coat a silvery
appearance. Her frontal fur, too, differs from the usual
white in being a distinctive creamy yellow.

In contrast with the forest red gums, blackbutts, and
tallowwoods of the gully, the only food trees now available are scribbly gums, and a blacktracker could easily have
followed her by the pits and straight scratches her claws
make among the zigzag scribblings of insect larvae on the
trees' silky gray bark. None of these gums, riven, twisted,
hollowed, and burned out as they are, is more than three
times the height of a man, and the little koala is absurdly
conspicuous by day, the sparse foliage offering no concealment whatever. But she does not sleep any the less soundly
for that, her ancestors over the ages having been pretty
safe as long as they were high enough above ground to be
out of reach of the dingo.

However, on one occasion, when feeding by daylight,
she attracts the attention of the pair of wedgetails whose
range includes the gully and the surrounding district. The
male comes down for a closer look and hangs awhile in the
wind, motionless and perfectly symmetrical except for the
sideways cast of his head. If the koala were on the ground
or even in a clear place in the tree, the eagle might have
attacked, and that would have brought him the immediate
support of his more formidable partner. But the scribbly
gum bristles with dead branches, some as sharp as spears,
and, in addition, the weight of the prospective prey—about
two kilograms—would be too much to lift, so the great

bird swings away and sails downwind, to disappear over the crest of the next ridge.

Three nights later the small Ishmael wanders into a town. It has been raining, and, puzzled by the glints and shadows made on the road by electric lights, she waits nearly too long and only just wins a race to the nearest telephone pole, which she ascends at a sort of vertical gallop. Although the few moments of violent action have certainly brought her to a pitch of complete alertness, an unusual state for her, she does not appear to be by any means terrified as she pauses to watch, bright-eyed, the leaping, clamorous dogs, and she is soon climbing on toward the wires and crosspieces gleaming in geometrical lines and angles against the black sky. It is when her front claws slide over a band of galvanized iron wrapped around the pole and continue to scratch helplessly at the metal that she starts to cry in the way that has repeatedly ripped human susceptibilities to shreds.

At last she becomes silent and motionless, except for sometimes turning her head to look down at the dogs. She is a pale gray blur in the glare of a moon too brazen ever to be dimmed by clouds or attended by a star. She is hanging by her arms, and though her talons are fixed into the tough, seamed wood of the pole, some effort is required to maintain her position. She is trapped and can do nothing but cling on while her strength lasts. She cannot save herself. Sooner or later she must fall.

In the morning she and the most optimistic dog are still there. There are also some people standing in the street and staring up. Somebody chases the dog away, which makes the onlookers feel better but does not greatly improve the situation. After a while some members of the Volunteer Bush Fire Brigade arrive with a ladder, and a man wearing leather gloves and carrying a corn bag manages, rather skillfully, to put the corn bag over the koala and then pull her free of the pole, thus capturing her neatly and without risk of being clawed by a terrified animal whose predominating instinct is to grab and hold on.

After a short time as a prisoner in a disused chicken coop, where she is given several kinds of eucalyptus leaves, she is called for by a ranger from the National Parks and Wildlife Service and released in due course in a suitable habitat.

This capture of a solitary koala in a region where no koala was thought to exist is just an example of how one of these small marsupials sometimes materializes out of nowhere; and many are the theories put forward by the interested to explain this phenomenon, the most popular being that the stranger has escaped from the collection of a fancier who is keeping protected animals in defiance of the law.

But the rangers of the Wildlife Service, the people called upon to rescue koalas when they are "treed" up telephone poles, found wandering about highways, or starving in suburban gardens, are usually able to reconstruct the history of the case in general, if not specific, terms. Always, they say, the koala is hopelessly bewildered. Either it has strayed away from a wild community or its habitat has been destroyed by clearing operations or by fire. To the question as to where in some particular region koalas could possibly exist, the reply is that pockets of bush remain here and there in rough country and in reserves. Admittedly, the great majority of the food trees that once flourished in developed areas have now been cut down, but the few that are left sometimes enable a koala to travel quite a long way by "island-hopping" from one feeding place to the next, until it reaches the end of the line. A town, farms, or grazing land where the last of the old eucalypts has died and the stock has trampled or eaten the seedlings—any of these can be the end of the line, and it was fortunate for the young female koala that her journeyings had led her to a town where she had been able to advertise the seriousness of her plight so appealingly and so dramatically.

There now being no more eligible females to mate with that season, and the weather being fairly mild, Boorana and the other mature males in the gully again turn their jealous attention toward their sons. They will continue for a while to suffer the presence of the younger ones, but the two eldest are particularly resented, just as their brothers and half-brothers were resented when they reached the unforgivable age. Occasionally, of course, a newly matured male may be lucky enough to acquire territory of his own, but, as this opportunity occurs only when an old male dies, the rule may be said to hold good that, in an isolated place where every scrap of the usable space is held, all the young males will be pushed right out of the area—most to starve in a hostile environment, a few, a very few, to be rescued and eventually released in another district by wildlife rangers.

Not quite as bulky as he was earlier in the breeding season, Boorana is probably the faster for that. Certainly he is able to gallop over the ground at a remarkable speed. But he is not as agile as the generation he so fiercely objects to, and is consistently outclimbed. Nor do his growlings and gruntings appear to have much of an intimidating effect. Indeed, both of his innocent enemies could have kept on outwitting and outclimbing him indefinitely, except for the fact that Boorana is their master in the art of descending a tree trunk, and it is not until the smaller of the two is backing down the towering shaft of a Sydney blue gum in order to cross to a blackbutt, whose greater size offers more scope for his nimbleness, that he finds his performance suddenly surpassed. He is, in fact, just completing his descent when his pursuer jumps from a lateral to the top of the smooth pillar of the blue gum and, with all four legs at full spread, whizzes down the straight trunk at a speed close to that of free fall. When he digs in his claws and rips to a stop, the old koala is so close to the fugitive that he almost lands on top of him. They dash away from the base of the tree in the selfsame second.

Overtaking his quarry at full gallop, Boorana bowls him along the ground, biting, clawing, and cuffing to the accompaniment of the harsh uproar of the one and the agonized outcry of the other as he strives to draw ahead, pummeled and scratched, no doubt, and somewhat knocked about, but in the main frightened rather than hurt.

So they go, the loser squalling his discomfort to the world, the victor lumbering far in the rear and gasping for breath now instead of giving tongue. Boorana comes to a halt at last and stands watching the outcast stumble wearily from the deep shadows of the gully and up the slope of the eastern ridge. He watches until, scarcely perceptible in the light of the new moon, the young male passes out of sight behind some rocks, and nothing moves except the sparse scrub of the hillside quivering in the wind, and there is no sound but the rustle of leaves above Boorana's head. Then the master of that territory turns back, his wide-set front legs with their great spreading claws picking their way carefully, his shorter, bandier back legs trotting self-consciously behind as though they knew they were the wrong ones, which had been hurriedly tacked on just before their owner had fallen off the production line, his tail still not added. When Boorana reaches the forest red gum, he does not begin his ascent by springing to a point almost his own height above ground but starts his climbing slowly, from the base.

Toward the end of February, about thirty-five days after impregnation, when the weather is hot again, the koala with the ragged ear produces her young, which this time completes its journey to her pouch. Ten minutes later the parent is climbing into the high branches.

As usual when dry westerly conditions prevail, the air smells of burning. The fires are on every side, the biggest, back in the timbered ranges, a huge conflagration which is sending up dense columns of smoke. Some of the others are nearly as big.

But big fires need big quantities of fuel, and when they reach the sandstone tops and ridges where the grandest trees are stunted, wind-torn angophoras and scribbly gums, the tall flames become small and run about the ground, scurrying along rock clefts filled with dead leaves and sputtering in dried bushes.

Talgara is the first of the koalas to sense imminent danger, though she cannot see any flames because of the high rim of the escarpment. But the smell of burning is different. It comes from fires closer by, and she descends from the eucalypt and canters anxiously to a turpentine tree. Her claws rasp loudly on its rough bark as she climbs, and she quickly disappears into its clustering leafage. She is very swift and agile, the scrap of life in her pouch still much too small to affect her movements. A wail of terror goes up from somewhere nearby—and no other animal but a koala could make such a sound.

The flames reach the edge of the escarpment before dawn and flicker decoratively about the rock's rim. Some of the hollows charred into the scribbly gums by the bush fires of other years begin to smolder again, and by morning the whole length of the escarpment is burning. A stream of coals tumbles over the cliff, and ripples of smoke start up from the grass below. Soon flames are crackling around the trunks of the trees in the gully.

That night the situation is one of continuing menace rather than of disaster. It seems certain now that the fire will not set the trees in the gully alight. The flames have died down, and the smoke from the burning grass is so thick that their brilliance has been somewhat dimmed. The koalas are not yet silent, but their cries have become less frequent. Coughing from the effects of smoke, Boorana climbs to the top of the forest red gum. After the slow westerly has carried the smoke away, the sparks and coals on the ground are like the lights of a city seen from a mountaintop.

Morning shows blackened earth; every stalk of grass and every bush has vanished, and the seedling eucalypts have been destroyed. The koalas are restless, though they feed from time to time. Talgara, in the turpentine tree, sleeps fitfully. Her young one is now about two and a half months old and as naked as the day he was born. But he is appreciably larger, though his form has not changed, except that his hind legs have developed sufficiently to look as though they may eventually grow into serviceable members. Enclosed within the equable humidity of his parent's pouch, he is safely insulated from the dehydrating effects of the fires and the wind.

When it is dark, Boorana comes down from his treetop and ambles toward a tallowwood close to the concentration of brush box and turpentines in the middle of the gully. Other koalas are changing from tree to tree now that the ground is cool enough to walk on, and Boorana is passed by the second of the young males approaching maturity, who is so anxious to give him a wide berth that he blunders into the red-hot base of a grass tree that has burned to ground level. As he jumps away, squealing with pain, the old male hits at him but does not follow up the opportunity to inflict further punishment. Exertion of every kind is to be avoided in the heat, and even the youngster, who is now clinging to a nearby trunk, does not climb far but hangs there, looking down over his shoulder to see what will happen next. But Boorana goes on, and a ragged-looking, ash-smeared creature he is.

Keeping three sets of his claws hooked into the bark, the young male koala raises his burned hind paw to the level of his eyes and peers at its upturned sole in a demonstration of the extraordinary range of his limb movements, which apparently is as great for his hind legs as for his front legs, or arms. Whimpering softly, he starts to climb, and because the injury is to that nailless and spatulate member his great toe—indispensable if the grip of the claws opposed to it is to be fully effective—one of his hind feet has been rendered temporarily useless. But his other limbs are so powerful that the restriction does not seem to affect his mobility in the slightest.

As soon as the wind shifts from the west, the weather becomes cooler, and Boorana roars his displeasure every time the second of the young males comes near him. But February ends with the conflict unresolved.

# MARCH

According to the calendar, it is autumn, but according to the weather, it is midsummer. However, there is a breeze to temper the heat as the koalas in the gully settle into the quieter part of their annual cycle. The female with the bloodwood stains on her fur gives birth early in the month, and Talgara's half-sister will follow suit in a few days.

Life for the koalas should then prove uneventful for a while, now that the breeding season is just about at an end. The mature females have mated, and no young female is within months of reaching the age when the process of separation of cub from mother is due to begin. It is true that one young male remains under the threat of expulsion, but the other male cubs—and there are several —have varying periods of untroubled living ahead of them

55

before they incur the jealousy of the holders of territory.

Boorana shares the contentment of his neighbors and rouses himself to growl angrily only when he becomes aware of the son he has so far been unable to frighten away. As a rule he sleeps solidly from sunrise to sunset, except for a brief interval of lazy feeding in the morning and another in the afternoon; and on occasion he may sleep on for two or three hours after dark, for his life, in common with the lives of other full-grown koalas in natural and undisturbed surroundings, is made up almost entirely of sleeping and feeding—at least, for eight or nine months of the year.

In the selection of sleeping places, every animal seems to have an individual preference, Boorana always choosing a massive junction, Talgara generally climbing out to a slim fork near the end of a lateral and never caring about the dangers of a wind-tossed perch, frequently not even bothering to grasp the branch. Other koalas may stay lower down, but, no matter where he sleeps, none of them ever regards any particular spot as a den or covert.

Though most koalas live in loose-knit communities, which may well owe their formation in the first place to the availability of food in a certain locality, and which usually remain fixed as long as the supply lasts, it is also true that many of them do become the drifters of the bushland. With the exception of the natural association of a mother and her dependent cub, two koalas seldom sleep, or even feed, in the same tree unless it is a very big one. Generally, they are happy to stay where they happen to be, as long as there is enough to eat and a little koala-free

space around them. Gregarious yet antisocial, they are occasionally, however, as contradictory in their behavior as
the platypus is in its appearance.

The days and nights pass evenly. As the furred and
feathered creatures of the gully seek out their food, there
are few evidences of their presence. True, the possums
sometimes stage a running fight through the branches, and
in the late afternoon wallabies may be heard thumping
down the eastern ridge to graze on the new shoots starting
from the tussocks of burned grass. But as a rule there is
quiet. Talgara's half-sister produces her young during this
time of calm. The one jarring interruption to the even
tenor of the lives of the koalas in the gully is the surprise
attack on the second of the young males.

Though the male koala in the territory adjoining Boorana's seldom changes trees between dawn and dusk, the
sun has been streaming so directly down upon him through
gaps in the leaves that he decides to move and, once
moving, keeps on going right to the ground, to stumble
sleepily over to a brush box; and it is here that the youngster is stretched out, in shade a considerable distance above
ground. If the sleeper hears the rasp of approaching claws,
he does not associate the sound with any danger to himself, for he has neither changed his position nor opened his
eyes when he receives a buffet that almost knocks him out
of the tree. However, he manages to save himself with a
grab that leaves him dangling until he gets his bearings.
Then he drops to the branch beneath. From there he
slithers down the trunk to the ground and blunders into
Boorana's territory. This move triggers such a furious out-

burst of threats that the youngster veers toward open country. And, though his retreat soon slows to a clumsy, lolloping canter, he does not pause but continues on, through the dazzling confusion of sunshine and shadow that makes the ground look as if it had been strewn with tiger skins, and on, stumbling now, right out of the gully into the full glare of afternoon. Even then, panicked by an onslaught that has come as the culmination of a long campaign of intimidation, the fugitive labors on toward the top of the slope.

When he has gone and there is silence, Boorana settles down as before, his eyes closed and his forearm pillowing his head. The koalas, all of them, are either deeply asleep or drowsing—even the young ones. As the day wears on, the breeze that had formerly been a cooling influence becomes as hot as the day. It is stronger, too, and has veered to the northwest.

From that evening, the story of March is the story of the elements rather than the story of koalas or of any other creatures.

Before morning the wind from the northwest has shifted again, menacingly, to due west. It is now a wind from out of the parched hinterland, a fierce wind that streams steadily over the escarpment and rakes the eucalypts so that their slim leaves vibrate horizontally in the blast. As the heat and dryness increase, some of the koalas come down from the eucalypts to seek the shade of the turpentine and brush box trees. When they are hungry they visit the tallowwoods, gray gums, forest red gums, and Sydney blue gums and return before daylight to the shade trees. Sunrise, and the westerly, which had abated slightly during the night, is again thundering through the treetops. The light flashes on the leaves, and no cloud can live in the wind-swept sky. Yesterday's glint of water seeping down the escarpment wall has vanished, and the new grass on the gully floor is being shriveled to the blackness of the burned tussocks from which it sprang. The wind tears at the small forest, which has now lost so much of its moisture that the noise of its foliage thrashing in the gusts has taken on a different, strident quality.

On the third day the westerly is as violent as ever, and the gully has become a firetrap. The safest place is the ground, where the earlier grass fire has consumed every-thing except the little that has blown down since. But the koalas stay in the trees. When, inevitably, the smell of burning comes, they cry out and climb higher. Scuds of smoke momentarily bedim the sunlight, and the terror of the koalas is as great as that of a troop of monkeys when they hear the cough of a jaguar. But they are helpless. When in danger from bush fires, they always climb higher, into the zone of maximum risk.

By this time many of the trees in the gully have had their moisture content so lowered by the onslaught of the westerly that they have become vulnerable to the point where the merest flicker of flame—even, perhaps, a spark —could set them alight. The eucalypts are especially flam-mable, some of their oil content having volatilized.

So it is a good thing, in a way, that the stunted vegeta-tion of the plateau behind the escarpment has been re-duced for the most part to charred stumps and heaps of ash. Yet, as always when fire passes through terrain where fuel is sparse, there are areas that have escaped unburned, and some of these are now being touched off by sparks from a huge blaze in the hills. Swathes of smoke from one such danger spot perilously near the gully, caught in a downdraft, are sliding over the rim of the escarpment like great gray pythons.

Then it happens. On the edge of the plateau a dead tree trunk, now transformed into a column of glowing coals, collapses in a flare of sparks, and a few moments later a cluster of eucalypts explodes. But the wind is so strong that the flames are blown straight across the gully and are gone, leaving a narrow strip of black sticks with smoke pennants fluttering. The body of a koala lies in the ashes underneath.

At intervals, in twos and threes, other eucalypts ignite; and each time the wind limits the spread of the fire by whirling the burning debris straight over the next ridge.

Temporarily blinded by wind and smoke, helpless and utterly bewildered, the koalas in the concentration of brush boxes and turpentines set up a terrified wailing. None of them moves except to peer with streaming eyes in one direction, then in another—yet quite unseeingly, to judge from the benumbed slowness of their head-turning.

The rocky escarpment to the west has been wholly burned out by now, and there are no more sparks to fly over the gully. That afternoon, when the sun is resting like a glowing coal on the top of the escarpment, the westerly starts to lose its force, and by nightfall, after the turmoil has died away, there is an unearthly silence and no breath of air. Smoke rising from debris on the ground is soon thick enough to hide anything not close by, though occasional red flickerings light up some of the lower branches as the bark of a tallowwood catches and a spitting little flame runs up the loose fibers of the trunk. Most of these fires flare and go out, but some may take hold and, by eating into the sapwood, make a breach in the tree's defenses for the next wildfire to rekindle and enlarge into a hollow that could eventually become as big as one of the black caves in the scribbly gums of the ridges.

The silence continues unbroken except for the coughing of the koalas, who are now hidden from one another in the dense smoke. Boorana is the worst affected. No other creature could possibly be responsible for the gruff raspings that emanate from the brush box trees.

Darkness that night is absolute until a breeze from the southeast springs up and gently blows the smoke away. The temperature falls too, as the humid sea air floods on toward the highlands. But the change will not cross the Great Dividing Range to cool the plains sweltering in the oppressive, breathless heat.

It is a cloudless night and not intensely dark, though there is no moon. It is a quiet night, with no bird calling and nothing moving except the surviving koalas, who are closer together than before and will remain so until the leaves grow again, for the effective size of the combined territories is less than half what it was.

Morning shows the desolation of the northern end of the gully. It also shows that some of the unburned trees have been seared by the heat, and that a cluster of eucalypts near the southern end is without a trace of green. With so much of their former leafy cover stripped away, the koalas are now cruelly conspicuous, especially where, as in the case of Talgara, they are perched out on laterals. The diurnal birds have not yet returned, and the only animals to be seen are the koalas and three gliders—the living and the dead. About twelve of the koalas have been killed; the bodies of the three gliders are huddled near the base of a blackbutt.

A female koala with a half-grown cub is sitting, erect and motionless, in a gray gum. One paw grips the forked branch in front of her; her hind legs droop limply. Nevertheless, she seems to be firmly positioned. She is staring straight before her. The fur on her neck and shoulders is singed. She has been shocked into a state bordering on insensibility and will die within two or three days, probably without moving from where she is. Her cub is asleep on her back. He is a big cub and old enough to be independent of his parent.

A short distance away, the head and forelegs of a brushtail possum hang from a spout in another gray gum, and here and there the bodies of koalas lie among the ashes on the ground. Although there must also be victims too small to be readily detected, it seems that none of the larger marsupials has been killed—other than the koalas, the brushtail possum, and the three gliding possums.

The gliders must have emerged from a hollow to obtain relief from the stifling heat of their refuge—a common practice with possums—and, similarly, the brushtail must have been making for the open air when a flying spark ignited the tinder-dry eucalypts. Death in the resultant explosion would have been instantaneous.

There is no color in parts of the gully. They are as austere as charcoal sketches. They look as though nothing will ever grow there again, while in some other parts the foliage has been so affected by the heat and the westerly that there seems to be another fire risk already, and one that will become more acute as the curling leaves shrivel to the brown of extreme flammability.

But if another spark is to reach the gully from any of the westerly directions, where the main dangers lie, it will now have to be carried over about thirty-five kilometers of desolation, a gap that can be bridged only by the combination of heat-wave conditions, a raging wind, and the updraft from a huge conflagration. With the month of March almost at an end, the colony is surely safe from a third visitation in the present year. Neither is the gully quite as sorely stricken as it would appear, because the effect of two fires in quick succession is usually less severe than that of a single holocaust, which can turn a forest into a desert. As it is, no mature tree has been killed, and soon most of the bare branches will be covered in green shoots. The weather is perfect. The temperature is moderate, the nights are calm, and the stars shine the brighter now that the last of the fires has burned itself out. Though the amount of food available in the gully has been reduced by about two-thirds, the leaves that have escaped the fires are fast regaining their moisture, and there is also dew in the mornings.

So the koalas quickly settle into a state of complete contentment. The breeding season well past and done with, they eat and slumber through the last, ironic days of March.

What matter if there are enough survivors to defoliate the biggest tree in the gully in a single night?—that is, supposing they were all to visit it at the same time. They are a somnolent, untroubled lot, and it is easy to imagine the last koala in Australia finishing off the last leaf of the last eucalypt and then, by chance being fully fed, curling up and going to sleep exactly as Boorana and the others do every morning.

So it is simply a question of whether the food will last until the burned branches can regenerate. New grass shoots to replace those blackened by the westerly will be first to appear, then the young leaves of the mature trees, and, months later, the seedling eucalypts. But none of these is to be seen as the month draws to a close in mild weather with balmy breezes and no rain.

# APRIL

Although the moon has set and there is no glint of dawn, the sky is brilliant. High up, the air is cold and clear. Yet occasionally a star flickers like a candle going out and then shines steadily again, for this is April and the migratory birds are flying north. So they pass in flocks, in phalanxes, and in echelons, golden plovers and whimbrels, sanderlings and sea curlews, their pipings and thin whistlings quickly fading as they sweep smoothly on through the bright arches of the night.

Below them the great rock slabs of the harshlands throw back a dim, pale light, and the burned areas are black pits. There are reflections too from huddles of living trees, mostly brush box and turpentine, though these are few and far between, and the country the bush fires have devastated is in the main not very different from the lifeless surface on the moon. Even the forest in the gully is not easy to pick out, for its shadows move only when a strong puff of wind reaches the few clusters of foiliage remaining.

The breeze in the eucalypts is a quiet and steady whispering, though in those places where the foliage has been scorched but not consumed it makes a faint crackling sound that is as much out of harmony with the softness of the night as is its droning through bare branches. Its voice is kindest, really, when, as in other, happier seasons, it surges around dark cliffs of turpentine and ruffles their leaves until they glint in the starlight like quick shoals of fish.

On such autumn nights, when to look up is to stare at a blaze of glory, there are other animals besides koalas to be seen in silhouette among the thinned-out foliage, for that part of the gully that was spared by the fires is at present somewhat overpopulated. Seven or eight tawny frogmouths and one rare and diminutive moth owl, all hunting for insects, are crowded into a very restricted space, as well as a pair of owls on the watch for marsupial mice and pygmy possums.

Besides the many former inhabitants left, there is also a number of newcomers, and every one of them is faring better than the koalas. Moths are fluttering about the newly grown grasses and the banksias, melaleucas, and callistemons, and consequently the frogmouths are the creatures most frequently in evidence as they float on silent wings to take an insect from the ground or a low branch. Their strange calls are like the muffled tapping of a drum and there is no sound louder than the hooting of the boobook owls and the occasional churring of the sugar gliders.

Of the various species surviving, the most active are the sugar gliders, but there are now fewer of these, those that are left being concentrated where the eucalypts suffered least. Though their diet normally includes blossoms and buds, they also eat insects and, as these are at present fairly abundant in comparison with other food, they pursue them with incredible agility and verve from dark till dawn.

Five in a family group living in a hollow branch not far from the brush box and turpentine trees have been hunting nearly all night long when suddenly they take it into their heads to play. The pace is dazzling. They could easily be mistaken for birds, they are so swift; and whether they are racing toward the stars or scampering headlong down a great tree trunk, the only sound is an occasional outburst of chattering like the starting and stopping of a clockwork toy. But now their shadowy forms, gliding membranes spread and long tails streaming, are following the leader from branch to branch in a series of the most prodigious floating leaps which are indeed neither leaps nor volplanes but a combination of both and none the less wonderful because a last and more sustained, slow-sailing dive takes the performers out of sight and leaves the human observer with the feeling that he has been peering into a dream world where impossibilities are the norm and there is no gravity.

Though these pixies of the bushlands have many enemies, they are by no means easy prey and thoroughly belie their gentle, soft-furred appearance, being as hardy as they are swift and as fierce as they are small—a blend of qualities that has enabled them to spread over the eastern arc of the continent from Darwin to Mount Gambier.

The bigger gliders—and there is still a mated pair of them in the gully—are almost as hard put to it as the koalas to find enough food to keep them alive, for, like the koalas, they are highly selective in their diet. But they are more mobile. And they are even more conspicuous as they climb through the leafless branches to a take-off point that will give them an unobstructed drop for the next glide. When planing through burned areas of the forest, they now lack that measure of concealment that had formerly been provided by the surrounding foliage, and there is no doubt that both would have fallen victims to the powerful owl whose territory included their own, except that this scourge of their kind, having been driven from his daytime refuge by the fire, is now sheltering and hunting back in the ranges some hours of flight away.

Many of the birds have left, and the wallabies are already far away, looking for new grazing land. Those tireless foragers the brushtailed possums and the lizards gradually disperse to every point of the compass in their search for food, and only the big gliders and the koalas seem to be absolutely fixed in their habitats—and in their habits.

Probably the animals least affected by the changed conditions are the wombats, who lumber down from their burrows in the eastern ridge at night to dig for roots between the trees and near the creek, where the ground is damp. They also eat the green shoots that appear on grass tussocks, which look like so many echidnas rolled up with their spines erect.

As the eucalypts that were not seriously damaged by the fires are denuded, one by one, of their most appetizing leaves, it becomes progressively more difficult for the koalas to pick and choose, and their occasional visits to the brush box and turpentine trees are not now to seek respite from the heat, for the weather is pleasant enough, but to satisfy their hunger. That reposeful, rather stolid attitude that distinguishes the grown members of the species in ordinary circumstances, once the breeding season is over, has changed to a restlessness that has been brought about not so much by uneasiness as by the obsessive search for the most palatable kind of food. The koalas are active but not agitated. There are plenty of older leaves, and these are quite edible, if somewhat tough and dry. The koalas eat them freely, but then move away in search of better fare. They seldom stay long in the same place, certainly not in the same tree. They are always seeking exactly what they want and often take serious risks to get it by edging out to the end of a lateral branch and by stretching to the point of overbalancing to gain a spray of leaves or to grasp at a slim branch above. Of course as the supply continues to diminish, these operations become more hazardous, as in every case another koala has been there before and has leaned over as far as he or she dared, so that the next comer, to be successful, must lean farther.

Naturally, Boorana is at a disadvantage in these ma-neuvers because of his weight, and twice the ends of laterals break to leave him swinging like a pendulum high enough above ground to be killed if he loses his grip. Fortunately for him and others of his kind, green branches never snap cleanly, and a moment's grace is sufficient for him to orient himself and to drop with superb aplomb to another branch or cluster of leaves below. Relieved of his weight, the broken end will swing in the breezes for months.

Falls do occur occasionally, and though many koalas, some of them fairly young, have survived impacts that would have been fatal to other animals, there are limits to what even these muscular little creatures can stand.

The ravens and crows that seem always to be crisscrossing the cloudless sky often settle for a while in the trees of the gully and send out their loud and raucous cries, their glossy throats swelling and the sunlight rippling along the curves of their black-satin plumage. These visits have become a habit—a habit that will not be continued for much longer, however, for there is nothing left for them in the gully. But, optimistically, they drop down yet again to pick at the remains of a glider so long dead that it is only bones and scraps of fur, or to forage briefly among the tree trunks, lurching rhythmically from side to side as they walk, for they are big birds and they have lived well since the fires. At last they beat up into the open air and over the harshlands.

There is no break in the spell of fine, mild weather, no variation of cloudless skies, and no sign of the eucalypts' coming into leaf again. Talgara's suckling will be four and

a half months old at the end of April and is now represented by a slight bulge across her body above the opening of her pouch. So far, he has known only darkness and
warmth and food. In a sense, he has not yet been born.
At any rate, he has not yet come into the world—or, when
he did, he immediately quitted it again for the security of
his parent's pouch. He is bigger now, of course, but still
attached to the teat, still blind, and still naked except for
a skimpy fuzz of fur on his body, still helpless. He is more
like a koala than he was when he was born—which does
not mean he was even remotely like a koala when he was
born. However, limbs are forming, and he is always stretching and kicking in the manner of very young animals.
So considerably has he grown that sometimes, when he
stretches, a pink and skinny leg may stick out of the opening of the pouch for a brief space before being drawn in
again. Obviously he has come to no harm from the combination of drought and bush fires that destroyed so many
of the wild creatures. Though Talgara must have suffered
severely from dehydration during that period, it is apparent that the humidity of her pouch was maintained.

Owing to the open nature of the forest—few branches
intermingle except where the brush box and turpentine
trees grow in the middle of the gully—the koalas are usually obliged to descend when they change trees. Before
the fire they were generally content to stay in the same
feeding place for long periods. Not so since, because of
the depletion of their food supply. Consequently there is
a lot of journeying back and forth, much of it fruitless as

far as any improvement in the quality of food is concerned, and they find themselves moving about much more than they would have otherwise.

Every time Talgara moves from one tree to another or, for that matter, from one branch to another, it is as though a shadow—a detached and floating shadow—moves too, as the male cub whose parent succumbed to the shock of the bush fire follows her. It is clear that he has come to identify her with his dead parent, though there is some evidence of awareness of a difference in the situation, in that he never tries to make contact with the substitute.

Talgara ignores him. He is neither encouraged nor repulsed. In fact he never comes close enough to be repulsed. This arrangement coincides approximately with the stage of separation that would have been reached by now if his own parent had lived, for the young koala is so well grown that he certainly would not have gained the coveted resting place on his dam's back on the day of the fire if she had not been too dazed to resist him.

Because his territory is so near the creek, now practically dry, Boorana sometimes calls there, not to drink but simply to nose curiously about its banks and, more rarely, to eat some of the damp earth, as certain animals do to overcome mineral deficiencies in their diet.

During this month of famine there is so much crossing and recrossing of the gully floor that it seems the koalas have turned into ground-dwellers. At one time they probably were, and when the sizable Boorana comes upon a wombat digging for roots and then himself starts to scratch some earth loose with his front claws, it could be said that he is side by side with a close relation—and a very ponderous relation, at that.

It used to be thought that koalas were a kind of possum that descended from the trees and then returned to an arboreal existence. Besides developing strong limbs during its stay in a new habitat, it was suggested, the koala had lost its tail, and also the opening to its pouch had moved from the top to a lower position, as in the wombats and other marsupial burrowers. In support of this theory, it was pointed out that the return to the trees must have been recent in terms of evolutionary time, as the pouch shows no sign of reverting to its alleged original design and the mislaid tail has not reappeared.

The discussion continues, and now that science has linked a number of features of koalas' blood, muscles, and spermatozoa closely with those of the wombat, it is generally believed that the koala was always a ground-dweller, perhaps a species of wombat, which took to the trees only yesterday—once again, in terms of evolutionary time. This explanation accounts most convincingly for the powerful limbs, the lack of a tail, and the position of the opening to the pouch, which, in an arboreal animal, does seem to be an inconsistency.

Not that there could ever be much danger of a cub's falling out, the pouch being a highly controlled, tough, elastic, and muscular organ, thoroughly capable of retaining its burden in all circumstances until the young koala is old enough to transfer to the parent's back.

Early on a morning near the end of this, the middle month of autumn, when the white rays of the moon are slanting through the burned trees at the edge of the gully, Boorana turns aside on one of the journeyings and again pauses at the damp place near the creek bed to scratch some of the earth loose and eat it. Close by, a wombat is feeding at the base of a clump of swordgrass.

Neither animal seems to have noticed the other—though of course each must be fully aware of his neighbor and of his harmlessness. Although the wombat is much larger than the koala, there is clearly a great similarity between them, even in an external and superficial way. Both are of stocky, powerful build and have the same shape of head and are tailless. Additionally, both have the same stout claws, though on closer examination the wombat's would be found to be blunted by digging.

In the setting of tree trunks as stark as the stems of giant ferns and illumined by moonlight unsoftened by the sway of foliage, it is as though time has rolled back to show two primeval creatures of the same kind digging for food along the margins of a dried-up watercourse.

As the month draws to a close, the conditions in the gully approach disaster level, and the koalas become increasingly restless. The range of their diet has widened. They now eat freely of the brush box, and Talgara spends much time in a Sydney blue gum, which she seldom visited when the leaves of other eucalypts were available. She also climbs the blackbutt again but immediately returns to the ground. The weather continues mild and cool, and nearly always clear. The trees look more ragged daily, and many of them have only a few inaccessible tufts of leaves left. Though the grass and some of the bushes of the gully floor are recovering, the forest is slower to regenerate, and so far no bud has appeared.

# MAY

The shadow of the escarpment climbs slowly up the rise to the east of the gully. It is already dusk in the hollows, but the ridge's rocky crest, excoriated by fire and brilliantly lit, is a confusion of fierce angles and strong earth colors heaped against the sky.

A young male koala in the top of a tall tree awakens suddenly and throws back his head to bring it within reach of the syndactylous claws of his hind foot. The combing of his coat, however, though vigorous at first, gradually becomes lazier until at last it stops. Head and hind limb sink slowly back to their positions of repose, and he is soon curled again into the ovoid form in which he sleeps. Gleams of sunset redden his fur and the highest rocks on the ridge in the same instant. A party of curra-wongs falls from nowhere into a tallowwood, its six or

79

seven members looking and sounding like twenty as they clamber over the branches hurriedly and noisily, anxious that one should not get the advantage of the others. As they are planing to the ground, a magpie scatters them, then, carried on by the speed of her dive, towers in a magnificent rising curve to carol briefly from the loftiest branch thereabouts—the meekest, sweetest songbird in the world.

Silence again. After a while the koala rouses for the second time and climbs to the fork above. It is almost dark. He peers around and, leaning out to the length of his foreleg, scents the air, drawing in drafts of it through his nostrils, craning his neck, and moving his head this way and that. He has awakened almost hourly through the day but has eaten only sparingly because most of the leaves near him are old and dried up, or diseased and half dead. Even those that are acceptable are only just so.

Apparently his investigation of the evening airs has told him nothing, and his descent is lethargic and without purpose. Nevertheless, his hunger drives him on down to the ground to follow a course that seems to be dictated by the obstacles he is obliged to avoid, for whenever he is turned aside he continues on in the new direction. He climbs another tallowwood but finds it eaten out except for the slender plumes of foliage he was unable to reach last night. But now he keeps edging closer, even though his support bends from the vertical to the horizontal before he can stretch out and break off the end to get at the leaves. It is a particularly risky maneuver in the present conditions, since there are only bare branches underneath to grab at if he should fall, and if a slim lateral bends too much, he swivels around to make sure his head stays higher than his rump. He is not equipped for down-climbing because he cannot alter the angles of his feet sufficiently for his talons to hook and hold irrespective of the position of his body. In this way he is far behind some of the possums and the gliders. And of course a koala does not possess a prehensile tail—though a brushtailed possum, having the ability to reverse the set of his hind feet, can stop, head down, on a smooth-barked tree at places where his tail cannot possibly be of any assistance.

So it is not only the weight of the larger animal and the lack of a tail that make it a somewhat inhibited climber. A koala can gallop up the trunk of a flooded gum almost as fast as any climber, but if he wishes to come down, he cannot come down head first—unless, by accident, he parts company with the tree. However, in an emergency and if the girth of the tree is not too great, he often resorts to the trick of slithering down, backward as usual, provided there are no projecting stubs or branches. Otherwise he must descend circumspectly, "hand over hand," and still backward.

Boorana, like the other koalas, is continually changing trees, sometimes making the transfer high up where their branches meet, sometimes by way of the ground. That night he visits a blackbutt. It is now the only eucalypt in the gully carrying a fair head of foliage, but the big koala, after sniffing at the bole, turns away and walks steadily up the rock-strewn slope of the ridge to the east, aiming directly into the breeze.

The going is rough, and he is soon dusted with ash.

There is no vegetation—only short, sharp spikes where bushes once grew, and the butts of scrubby trees. His talons rasp and slide beneath him, and he is panting before he gains the top. In front of him is another down-slope, then another up-slope and, as the moon sails gloriously across a chasm in the clouds, both sides of the hollow are checkered with gleaming rocks and black shadows. Gradually the difference between the speed the traveler makes uphill and the speed he makes downhill becomes more marked, and he is asleep by midnight in a fallen scribbly gum. He is hungry too, as well as tired, but already proving to be of tougher fiber than most informed people would give koalas credit for.

Behind him, Talgara and the young male whose parent died a few days after the fire are just now leaving the gully, he being drawn after her as though she were his mother.

Although Talgara would not be plodding in the wake of Boorana if there were any food left in the neighborhood, it does seem that there is some slight affinity between them. She seldom moved far away from his territory when living in the gully, though every female is always free to come and go at will as far as males are concerned; and she is at present following him due east. But due east also happens to be the quarter from which the breeze is blowing, and there is little doubt that her keenness of scent, like his, has detected a hint of forest land in the same direction as the green paddocks near the coast—a hint so subtle that probably only the natural and well-schooled competence of a koala could recognize it.

It is only from the east, of course, that any encouragement can come. There is nothing but the bitter tang of wood ash to be blown in from anywhere else, though the north and south have not been quite as badly affected as the west, where desolation stretches right back into the ranges. So the female koala is traveling the same way as Boorana because she too is able to read the message of the east wind—yet it is also true that she is taking exactly the same paths as he and climbing the low cliffs by the same faults and fissures. Even so, if the breeze were to swing around and bring the scent of food, say, from the south, she would immediately swing away in that direction.

Boorana, she, and the young male are the only animals to quit the gully that night. She is more agile than Boorana and negotiates the roughnesses of the terrain with less trouble, often, where the going is easier, breaking into a canter. Her suckling of four and a half months old is not yet a burden and, being attached as firmly as ever to the teat, has no knowledge of any other sort of world than the warm and comfortable darkness of his mother's pouch, where there is nothing to do but to accept as much as he can of an unfailing supply of milk.

Talgara passes the big male koala asleep in his fallen scribbly gum and keeps going in the same line, with her tired "shadow" a long way back and losing ground. Morning finds them in the wreck of an angophora, both as black as the charred limbs of the tree. Never before have their intestines held so little food, and Talgara is on the move again by midafternoon. If the young koala following her had been a month older, he might have slept on, and, if he had slept on, he might never have awakened. But the urge to keep close to the female he has substituted for his parent is sufficient to rouse him, and he starts to walk again. Every now and then he sets up a crying sound, but Talgara does not slow, and when she suddenly veers away and quickens her pace, so does he, cutting across to shorten the distance.

Growing in a gap between rocks is a scribbly gum that has completely escaped the flames. Even the brittle debris around its base is unburned. Sparks of light glint from the living foliage waving against the stars as the koalas start to strip the tree, not troubling in their haste to allow each other room to move. Yet Talgara shows no antagonism or impatience, though, in the first minutes of feeding, the starving young koala who has trailed her for so far and so long is always in the way, stretching over her or under her and often grabbing at the same leaves.

Guided by the same uncanny sense of smell that led Talgara to the place, Boorana arrives before dawn and makes for the thickest remaining head of foliage. On the way up he climbs over the cub as though the youngster were part of the tree.

The scribbly's store of leaves, never abundant, has been reduced to half its original size by sunrise, but apparently two of the wanderers are satisfied. The third and biggest of them feeds on into the morning and then, with the others, throughout the following night. They finish the last of the leaves before the dawn of the second day and quit the tree in the afternoon, when they head east as before. Boorana's nose with its pink end markings keeps lifting as he walks.

The distance to their next target is covered in twenty minutes, and, though there is not an unburned stick on the way, the depression in the rocks from which the scent of eucalyptus is emanating has a number of trees—the inevitable scribbly gums, some gray gums, smooth-barked angophoras, and a Sydney peppermint. Water trickling from under a ledge has filled a pool from which there is no visible outlet.

Boorana crashes boldly through the thin understory of bushes and climbs a gray gum. Talgara chooses the Sydney peppermint, the least stunted of the eucalypts, but the young male, like Boorana, prefers a gray gum.

During that day, when the breeze becomes a wind from the southwest, the three koalas are once more screened by waving, rustling leaves. But as the movement of air is now from the wholly devastated areas, the koalas abandoning the community gully that night do so entirely without purpose, and the exodus becomes haphazard, with animals heading for every point of the compass except west, where the escarpment is an impassable barrier. Of those setting out in the same direction as that taken by Boorana, most will turn aside sooner or later, for they have nothing but the smell of a scorched land in their nostrils. Behind them, their gully habitat will slowly recover, but, unless man intervenes, it will never know another koala.

Yet it is almost impossible for such poor country as that which lies around the gully ever to be completely destroyed by a single fire, and some of the earlier burns are already showing a tinge of green. The koalas wandering north eventually come upon one of these places, though in this case the process of regeneration is not sufficiently advanced to provide enough food for even one of them.

The first to arrive is a female with an "embryonic" cub in her pouch. She eats some new shoots that have scarcely broken through the bark, and noses about in search of more.

Two more koalas—an old male, formerly a holder of territory in the gully, and an immature male—reach the same area soon after sunrise and begin foraging through the weird, dead-looking maze, each blackening his muzzle in nipping off the tiny leaf buds glistening against the charred wood. It is tiring work, with much labor involved in the winning of a mouthful, and the old male gives up after a while and goes to sleep on a fallen tree trunk. It is his last sleeping place. Though he awakens or appears to awaken on a number of occasions, he never tries to move away or to feed again. He is the fourth of the six males who held territory in the gully to die as a result of the fire; only Boorana and one other now survive.

The young male dies the next day, the female and her empouched young a couple of days later. None of them shows any evidence of distress or really rouses again from the sleeping posture, except that at one stage the young male comes down to search for water and, finding none, returns to a place above ground, where he curls up for the last time.

Whatever the ultimate total of losses from the fires, the chances of survival of the few koalas who have reached the

depression with food trees on the eastern edge of the harshlands have obviously greatly increased, though their lives
in the cleared and semi-cleared lands they are now approaching will be lived in very different conditions from
those they have been used to.

It has also become apparent that the number of koalas
to die from one or more of the secondary results of the fires
is higher than the number killed outright—which seems to
indicate that the reports of widespread epidemics in the
past may have been based upon a wrong conclusion, especially as the reports of the worst epidemics generally coin-
cide with the years of the worst bush fires.

It may now never be known whether the great bush fires
and the reports of epidemics were really connected. Many
informed people argue that koalas just do not escape from
bush fires. Certainly no animal is more helpless at such
times, and it is an indisputable fact that multitudes of
koalas died in the terrible wildfires that swept the land. But
fires sometimes do freakish things, and so do koalas; and,
though the proportion of those who escaped incineration
would be microscopic in comparison with the proportion
who suffered that fate, the finding of even a few unburned
bodies in nearby unburned, though unsuitable, country
would have been enough to give the impression that these
were the victims of an epidemic, whereas death may have
been caused by shock, by the continued eating of harmful
food, by straight-out poisoning, or by starvation.

In the case of poisoning, the initial recovery growth of
some eucalypts must be held suspect, especially if the animals feeding there have been in a state of near-starvation

for some days—as were the three koalas from the gully when they came upon the burned-out but regenerating piece of scrubland. It will never be known what part, if any, the new growth played in their deaths. But in another and allied field it is known that the feeding of eucalypt loppings to sheep during drought has repeatedly resulted in heavy loss of life—though, to make confusion worse confounded, cattle do well on the same diet. Perhaps certain poisonous qualities found in the new growth of some fire- or drought-damaged trees, which, in some instances at least, are strong enough to affect sheep, are also nature's defense against browsing animals when the quick production of leafage becomes imperative for the trees' survival.

Koalas' feeding habits and susceptibilities in general are not fully understood, one of the best-known quirks of the animal's behavior being as much a mystery today as it was when first observed: a sudden refusal to eat any more of the foliage of some particular eucalypt it has been feeding on for months. Gourmets, of course, will say that the answer is obvious, but most scientists suspect an abrupt and drastic, probably poisonous, change in the chemical composition of the leaves.

Talgara experienced a revulsion of this kind when she left the blackbutt tree in the gully which she had been feeding on occasionally by day, never to go back to it. And there is a reversed example of the same kind of thing in the behavior of the koalas at Koala Park, near Sydney. Why is it that for most of the year none of the koalas penned for exhibition will touch the leaves of a eucalypt known locally as "gray box," of which there are two specimens in the grounds; yet if the foliage is cut and given to them when their kinsmen at large in the park are feeding in the gray box trees, the penned koalas will eat it too? It is noteworthy that when leaves are rejected they are usually rejected without tasting, apparently on scent alone.

Although the food trees in the depression where Boorana, Talgara, and the young male are at present situated do not undergo any chemical change while the koalas are there, the number of grown animals dependent on them has been increased to eight by the arrival of five more from the gully, with the result that the value of the place as a harborage has been reduced almost to the level of the harshlands surrounding it. The gray gums look as though they have been stripped by locusts, small branches have been broken from the scribbly gums, and there are considerable gaps in the Sydney peppermint.

Rain, driven by a south wind, seems to inhibit the uneasiness of the indwellers temporarily. Curled up in trees by now almost leafless, they look like so many strange round fruits as they bob and sway with the swaying branches. Not one of them changes shape by so much as the twitch of an ear, but all have turned away from the weather. Their backs have a bedraggled appearance.

Talgara seems to be asleep. Her youngling, though still anchored to the teat, has grown rapidly through the latter part of May. He is now nearly five and a half months old and recognizable as a small koala, with a head elongated rather than broad. His fur is fine, soft, and sparse. He is able to open his eyes, but they are mostly closed, even during his spasms of energetic kicking. Except when asleep, he is nearly always moving his legs, in preparation for his eventual emergence from his mother's pouch into the eucalyptus-scented air of an Australian bushland night. Not that every part of the Australian bushland is scented with eucalyptus. It is just a guess that his mother will be chewing eucalyptus leaves in a eucalyptus tree when he so emerges.

With her back turned to the weather, her head bowed over her frontal fur, and forelimbs folded, Talgara would have had no difficulty in keeping her offspring dry even if he were old enough to be sitting in her lap. In the position he now occupies, he is doubly insulated.

Although the wind and rain show no sign of abating, two of the koalas bestir themselves as a gray gleam in the east widens to reveal the whole gray landscape. Descending from their different trees, which are some distance apart, both make the same vigilant pause as they near the ground and then independently walk directly into the wind. They chance to be roughly abreast and about ten meters apart.

Both are females with "embryonic" young, and they travel so straight that they must know there are eucalypts ahead. They seem to know too that the supply is not far away, for there is an eagerness about them that is quite evident.

Boorana waits some hours before moving. When he does decide to go, the light is as cloud-obstructed as ever, the wind as strong, and the rain as heavy, the spray of its downpouring illumining the streaming rocks. Cats'-paws race across shallow pools of floodwater, but Boorana plods through everything at a rate rather better than his ordinary pace. His demeanor is very like that of the pair that preceded him and results in the same directness of course, the same bullheadedness of purpose, the same look that he, as they, would prefer to go over an obstacle or through it, if that were possible, rather than be turned aside even momentarily; and there is the same complete disregard of the elements.

Head down, drenched, he splashes on at a good rate. But he is not built for speed, and his gait soon becomes more ungainly than it was when he started out. As he wades from a deeper pool, with the water pouring off him and his fur slicked close, another truth becomes apparent. He is a lean animal with narrow, almost skinny, flanks. Once again his belly is nearly empty—and he has scant reserves of strength. Shortness of breath afflicts him, and suddenly he stops. He goes on again after a while and then stops again, surprisingly to lap at a puddle of rainwater.

But his journey from the gully in search of another food supply is nearly over, and soon he is climbing into a thicket of eucalypts. He cannot be any wetter than he is already, but every grab he makes at the leaves around him brings down another shower.

Talgara is the next-to-last of the eight to set out on the final stage of the pilgrimage to a new land. She is followed at a distance by the young male who has substituted her for the image of his parent—a one-sided illusion if there ever was one.

Making more speed than any of the others, Talgara breaks into a canter in response to the strengthening scent of eucalyptus, and the little creature behind similarly increases his pace. They approach the forest of native trees just where its gray-green wall of foliage is dwarfed by a line of pines. There is a house close by, and the koalas are checked by an outburst of barking and the rattling of chains.

Running from under the veranda of the house, a cattle dog comes into view, silent, head held low, moving as smoothly as a fox. The uproar in the background continues. Talgara, intercepted, waits, stiff-legged. As the dog closes in, she raises a front paw, talons widely spread. The dog circles, then races in, and she hooks him. He accepts the sting without protest but backs off with such haste that his paws slither in the mud. A wash of blood and rainwater spreads across his muzzle. The young koala makes a dash for the eucalypts and gains them. Talgara retreats too, but is careful to keep facing the enemy. Next, the dog rushes and sheers off. He is as dangerous as ever and as determined, but she is something new in his experience. As soon as she comes into contact with the trunk of a tree she sits down and leans against it, and now she has both front sets of talons for defense. Every time he moves in she dabs at his eyes. It is a stalemate. He does not care to press the attack, and she knows that to try to climb the tree would be to present her unguarded back.

Then the young male koala claws his way to a higher branch, and the dog's attention is momentarily distracted. Talgara takes her chance and streaks up the tree with all the speed her heavily muscled limbs can supply. Eight koalas, three of them females with empouched young, have reached the safety of the strangely uniform little forest.

That day the gale veers to the southeast and, sharpened by the chill of winter, lashes the small trees relentlessly.

Dark gypsy clouds, torn by the wind, traipse endlessly in from the coast and over the hillside, their ragged skirts trailing, nor could any other kind of weather so pointedly illustrate the wild nature of the koalas and their consonance with the elements. They are like the forest itself in that the rain falls and the winds swirl and they do not seek shelter. Sometimes one stares uncomprehendingly at the yellow-lit windows of the farmhouse.

Years ago the house was surrounded by well-grassed paddocks with clumps of shade trees; then the farm was abandoned. In less than a couple of seasons, a host of seedlings had appeared, mostly eucalypts, with thickets of wattle and some turpentines. As there was no stock to trample them or to feed on them, they grew to be more than saplings but less than mature trees.

Now the rundown property has been sold. Fences and gates have been renewed, a tractor has started plowing, and the area of second growth has been marked down for clearing before the trees become too big to be knocked over by a bulldozer.

When the weather is calm again, the moon shows the expanse of young eucalypts to be wide enough to stretch from the line of pine trees near the house to the misty limits of sight.

# JUNE

The forest of second-growth eucalypts covers an area of about five hundred by three hundred meters, the whole sloping gently toward a gully so steep-sided that its edges have been taken as a sensible limit for the clearing operations now being negotiated.

Many of the small trees of the hillside are represented in the gully, but on a rather different scale. Down there huge blackbutts dominate the scene, though some of the tallow-woods and bloodwoods are almost as big; and another kind of eucalypt, the flooded gum, thrusts up its slim, pale shaft. Singly and in groups the flooded gums stand so straight that they give the impression of having risen from the forest's floor to sunlight in a day's growing. Yet it is no wonder that they are magnificent, for their roots are

95

deep in soil continually enriched by a rain of leaves that has been falling for a thousand years.

Though most of the great eucalypts are also food trees of varying degrees of acceptability, none of the koalas visits them, probably because the sunny verges of the forest are thick with privet and lantana, two exotics which find the climate of eastern Australia so completely to their liking that they soon overwhelm the native bushes and seedling trees in competition with them. In some districts they also act as a considerable check on the movements of koalas, who have a pronounced dislike for walking through dense undergrowth even when there is a track, which in this case there is not.

Not that any of the eight newcomers has made what might be called a determined attempt to travel farther east. Their present habitat seems to suit them very well. It is certainly ideal for the two mature males, who have both been able to acquire territory merely by being there. Nor do they come into conflict with each other, since their territories do not adjoin. Of course, if the locality had already contained a community of koalas, neither of the full-grown males would have been in his present state of comparative contentment but would still have been fighting for a foothold or else have been driven away. As it is, they have already settled into an environment where they are in the sort of situation most natural to them—not quite solitary, not exactly gregarious. Having attained this position with a minimum of stress, they suffer from none of the effects of shock.

All the koalas in this group are now scattered across the

whole area and, with the exception of the two mature
males, wander widely every night. But because of their
nocturnal habits and their silence when they are not in the
breeding season, as well as the amount of protection the
thick leafage affords them by day, their presence remains
undetected for a while and would have continued so except for Talgara's predilection for sleeping in the tallest
tree within range.

It has taken her two weeks to get used to the barking of
dogs at night and the clashing of their chains, but slowly
these sounds have come to mean less, until in the small
hours of a clear morning she works her way through the
tops of the trees to the edge of the space around the house.
Here the lowest branch of a pine tree is almost within grasping distance, but not quite. The long, sweeping branch
rakes the stars, a keen pre-dawn breeze rustles the eucalypts, and the house is as black and as silent as a boulder.
Beside it a white, unblinking star shines from the metal-
work of a tractor. The koala backs halfway down the tree
trunk and pauses to look down over her shoulder in characteristic manner, listening and scenting the air. To judge
from the cast of her head and her slow peerings this way
and that, she is anything but keen-sighted. Her claws rasp
on the bark as she resumes her descent, but the sounds
raise no alarm, and in fact there is no other sound at all
except the cry of a spur-winged plover in flight overhead.

Evidently Talgara has her share of that peculiar brand
of nonaggressive daring which seems to be present in most
koalas, for she suddenly drops to the ground and ambles
boldly into the open, making no attempt to take advantage

of any cover that might be available, or to hurry, or to walk quietly, simply moving straight ahead and springing to the base of the nearest pine tree. As she climbs, she uses the great strength of her legs to keep her body slightly clear of the tree, for the young one in her pouch is now big enough to be bumped against the stubs on the lower part of the trunk. That this is the loftiest tree in her experience does not deter her from going right to its top, to its highest lateral, where there is no avoiding the wind or the sun or rain —or eventual detection. Below her, a streak of yellow light spears from the farmhouse.

Talgara takes no grip of the branch she is sitting on, though one of her hind feet rests against the stalk of the tree—it is not a trunk at that height, or even a stem. Her front limbs are folded, her head is bent, and she is asleep in a position that can only be described by a human being as terrifying. The wind sways the slender top of the pine tree and stirs the short, soft fur of the koala as darkness drains from a world tilting slowly east.

Talgara does not stir until afternoon, and then only because she is cramped from being so long in the same position, but the movement attracts the attention of two miners —noisy miners—who come wriggling up from the depths like fantailed goldfish through clear water. It is only once in a while that they visit the lofty zone formed by the tops of the pine trees, so the koala is not really trespassing on their territory—except that everywhere seems to be their territory. A patch of bare yellow skin behind each eye gives the pair an odd appearance. Though weak fliers and not formidable by any standard, they are often successful in chasing away larger and stronger enemies because of their readiness to band together, and soon all the members of the local gang are swirling about Talgara, uttering their shrill yapping cries and sometimes alighting on her back and pulling her fur. Finally, defeated by her unresponsiveness, they retire, but not before the disturbance and the cause of it have been noted by the farmer's son and his friend. They move this way and that, trying to get a better view. The farmer's son, who has a good knowledge of most of the local native mammals, says it wouldn't be a possum sitting up there like that—and it couldn't be a koala.

"Why couldn't it?" his friend asks, twitching back his snowy hair. He doesn't reckon Jim knows such a lot about animals, anyway. "I haven't ever seen a koala, only in pictures, but in my opinion it could be."

"Not here it couldn't."

"Why couldn't it?"

" 'Cause there aren't any."

Silence. Then the farmer's son concedes a point. "Well, it might be. Only it wouldn't be up a pine tree. They only eat gum leaves."

"It could come down at night. There's tons of gum leaves around."

At that moment Talgara uncurls and stands up, makes as though about to move, then settles down again in the same place. There is no longer room for doubt, and the rest of the afternoon is spent in watching her through field glasses.

A telephone conversation that evening between the

farmer and a wildlife ranger brings the information that where there is one koala there are probably more and that the animal in the pine tree may be a refugee from the recent bush fires. But the ranger has no equipment available for climbing pine trees such as the one described, and, even if he did, he would not feel too happy about taking on the job at his age, especially if the koala is right up in the small branches. When he calls in later, on his way to Sydney, he learns that a second koala, a bigger one, has been seen and that the farmer is anxious to have the area searched before the clearing contractors arrive at the end of the month. He feels that the ranger's guess about refugees from the bush fires is correct and that there may be other koalas in the eucalypts scheduled to be destroyed.

When the position of Talgara is pointed out to him, the ranger asks the farmer to release his dogs that night after the koala has come down to feed. If one of the dogs is then chained to the base of the pine tree and the others left at large, the capture could probably be made in the morning without risk or trouble. Unfortunately, Talgara does not remain near the edge of the clearing around the house when she discovers her return to the pine tree has been cut off, but wanders back into the eucalypts.

After this disappointment, the catching project is postponed until the ranger returns in a few days. In the meantime the boys will make a count of the koalas on the property. However, once again the result is poor, only one animal being found, and that is Boorana, who now sleeps every day in a particular tree within his new territory.

So the party of three—the ranger and the two boys—
sets out, and there, sure enough, in his usual place and
looking too heavy for the gray gum sapling supporting him,
is the big male koala.

Footsteps, whispered directions, and the crack of a stick
awaken the koala, and he peers down sleepily. But he does
not move until the ranger places a ladder against the tree
and starts to climb. Boorana climbs too. The tree is not
tall, and, balancing on the ladder's highest rung, the ranger
tries to seize the koala. A taloned forepaw stops him, and
now Boorana starts to roar in his harsh, grunting voice. His
posture and demeanor have changed. He looks bigger,
leaner—and meaner. The ranger steps onto a branch for
firmer support, and Boorana leaps clean out of the tree and
into the next one. He loses a lot of height, but it is a powerful spring none the less, and the watching boys cannot
help ducking as the gray-brown shape at full stretch hurtles
overhead.

Boorana lands sloppily in a mass of pendent foilage, and
while he is swinging there the ranger places the ladder in
a new position and manages to grab his quarry by the scruff
of the neck. Hauling Boorana out of the tree, he holds him
at arm's length—no mean feat, considering the captive's
weight and furious struggles. Koalas have practically no
loose skin anywhere about their bodies, and the heavy animal is being cruelly pinched. His roarings rise to a tremendous pitch, and his hooked, needle-sharp talons flail
dangerously for a grip—a grip of anything, wood or flesh—
to ease the strain. However, nothing can be done for him

until the man is back on the ground, when he puts his free hand under Boorana's rump, and the emotional content of the performance evaporates.

Having carefully instructed his helpers on how to hold a canvas bag wide open and clear of the ground, the ranger throws Boorana backward into it, thus avoiding the desperate business of trying to push a sizable animal in frontward when it is all claws and agitation.

With the koala safely imprisoned and not greatly frightened or knocked about—he has been rather cheaply taken—the party begins the search proper. And the search proper becomes a more definitely hopeless business the longer it goes on; and it goes on and on under a winter's sun that gets steadily hotter down there in the thickets of eucalypts. They find nothing until quite late in the afternoon, when the ranger spots a koala in silhouette against a patch of sky. As they approach, they see another. Both are watched while one of the boys goes back for the ladder.

The smaller of the two discoveries, a young female, is captured with ridiculous ease. She is so amenable that the ranger, part way up the ladder, checks her by stroking her shoulders and back and, when she turns to look at him, lifts her out of the tree. He holds her against his shirt, facing him, as he comes down the ladder.

In spite of a mild objection from the farmer's son, the docile little creature is also put into a canvas bag. Although the other koala has not changed her position, she is fully alert and springs into the next tree before the ranger gets near her. Nor does she shrink from some considerable downward leaps, and it is obvious that her occasional slitherings and seeming missteps do not greatly affect her agility or speed. If one foot is not quite accurately placed, there are always three more furnished with talons as sharp and strong as climbing irons.

She eventually gets herself onto the end of a long lateral, from which there is nowhere to go. A saw is passed up to the ranger, who cuts just deep enough for the branch to drop as if on a hinge. The two boys throw a wide mesh net over the koala and hold her firmly enough to prevent her from climbing the swinging branch. She cries out at intervals but seems bewildered, and the ranger has no trouble in completing the capture.

Counting himself fortunate to have located and procured three koalas out of the massed eucalypts, and the shadows now having merged into semi-darkness, the ranger brings the search to an end, in spite of an assurance from his helpers that there is at least one more koala, Talgara, to be found. Besides, there is more work to be done before he leaves to keep an appointment, early next morning, forty kilometers the other side of Gloucester.

Back at the farmhouse, in failing light, the three koalas are weighed in their respective bags and their net weights recorded. They are also tagged for future identification. Boorana becomes N.W.P.S. 86M, according to the red plastic tag fastened through his left ear. His weight is 9.2 kilograms, which is fairly heavy for a male koala from the mid-coast of New South Wales. His struggles increase while the wear on his molar and pre-molar teeth is being assessed. The cusps of the pre-molars have been ground down to the same level as the molars, but he has lost no teeth and they are all sound. The information is noted. Boorana's age is reckoned at six years.

By taking turns holding the torch during this examination, the boys obtain a clear picture of the arrangement of the four pre-molars, sixteen molars, and eight incisors, six of which are on the upper jaw and only two on the lower. A pair of degenerate canines on the upper jaw are so insignificant that they are difficult to see while the animal is struggling, so the ranger allows each boy to feel their needlelike points with the tip of a finger. Though no longer of use, they bring the number of teeth to thirty.

The weight of the mature female, now tagged N.P.W.S. 87F, is 5.3 kilograms, and her age about four; while the young female weighs 2 kilograms and is reckoned to be sixteen months old. She is given number N.P.W.S. 88F. No measurements are taken by the ranger because of the inexperience of his helpers. However, a bulge in the pouch of the mature female betrays the presence of a young koala, which he supposes to be attached to the teat, though the mother fights him so furiously when he tries to make sure that at last he gives up. June being not yet far advanced, it is pretty certain that the young one would be less than six months old.

Both full-grown koalas are now so agitated that the use of some kind of tranquilizer might well be thought advisable; this method is generally used to ease the suffering of fierce or nervous animals under constraint. But koalas, being small enough to be quickly overpowered and held without injury, seldom show evidence of serious ill effects, provided they are not kept in confinement for a long period and are released in natural and peaceful surroundings.

In the present instance, of course, release cannot be effected immediately, which prompts the farmer's son to wonder whether the young female koala can possibly survive the journey into the northern part of the state. He is assured by the ranger that she will fare better than either of the full-grown captives, but that the sooner he moves, the sooner all the prisoners will be freed.

So, with the parting request that he be informed if any more animals are located, he loads the koalas into the back of his four-wheel drive, thanks his helpers, and starts the motor. Rolling out of the yellow glow from the house's side door, the truck fades into indistinctness down the bush track; the rattling of its aluminum ladder and other gear dies away; its lights flicker through the trees and disappear.

"You could probably be bitten by a koala, if you weren't careful," the farmer's son observes. "Judging by their front teeth. Anyway, Mum says stop and have some tea." And they walk indoors.

The captives wobble gently on a bed of cut branches, but the noise and the vibration of the motor come through with, every now and then, a bone-shaking concussion. Although the even tenor of the earlier part of the month of June has ended, those two weeks of tranquillity—fine mild weather, good feeding, and the complete absence of harassment—have enabled the refugees to recover some of the strength lost during their exodus and will increase their chances of living through such stresses as may be in store for them, especially in the case of Boorana, the least adaptable of the three, whose comfortable existence as a possessor of territory has again been blown to shreds. It is mainly because of concern for the biggest and strongest of the three prisoners that the ranger has no time to spare. He reckons the young female of about sixteen months will not be greatly affected by her experience and that the older female will also survive, but that the big male will have a fair chance only if he is released promptly and not too severely chivvied by other males already holding territory. The ranger considers twenty-four hours to be the limit of confinement for a fully grown wild koala—and mature males are likely to die in a shorter time than that, generally without notice.

The ranger arrives at the meeting place at peep of day, having left Gloucester in darkness. Sunshine is shafting through the trees, and it is pale gold except where the smoke of a campfire drifts toward the high branches when he strolls over to a loggers' camp to learn that a party of men has been on the site yesterday and the day before. They said they wanted to move the koalas out before the trees came down.

"How many did they catch?"

"Didn't catch any." The logger cannot quite hide a smile as he swills the dregs of tea around in his billy and tosses them out. "They only spotted one, an' he was way up in the top of a dirty great bloodwood."

"Did they say they'd be back?"

"One cove's coming back. Said he had to meet a bloke today. Wildlife ranger. Think they want some suggestions."

Involuntarily, the ranger glances up. The other moves

away. "There's some big trees around here, all right," he adds. "Some of the biggest I've seen. Well, I got a few things to clean up. We'll be starting to knock 'em down tomorrow." Then he pauses and turns. "Listen, mate, I'd like to see the koalas taken out too, before the gang gets going, but what can you do? There's always animals killed when clearing has to be done. Can't avoid it, I've never been able to work anything out."

The ranger nods. "It's a pretty big forest, this one," he admits.

When the spokesman for the unsuccessful catching party arrives, it is arranged that a volunteer be asked to be present when the tree-felling starts, in order to take possession of any koalas brought down and to transfer them to the nearest natural bush thought suitable. The ranger himself cannot wait to assist, as his own charges have already been held for fourteen hours and must now be released as quickly as possible. To let them go in wild bushland, where they would almost certainly never be seen again, would be to cancel out the value of the information he has recorded about them as tagged animals, and therefore he presses on toward Lismore and the National Parks and Wildlife Reserve nearby, at Tucki Tucki, and sets them free there, twenty-seven hours after their capture.

Some of the eucalypts in the reserve are original bush trees, but most have been planted by hand, forming an open woodland about the same age and height as the second-growth forest where the koalas were caught. When the youngest of the three, N.P.W.S. 88F, is placed in a forest red gum, she twists her head around to stare curi-

ously at the man for fully a minute before climbing unhurriedly out of reach, but the mature female wastes no
time in disappearing into the high foliage of a tallowwood.
Only Boorana seems at a loss. Every rasp of his claws on
the bark of any tree brings a protest, sometimes grumbling,
sometimes fierce, and when the ranger leaves, he is back
on the ground. It is a pity, the man reflects, that he was
unable to complete his journey in daylight, before the
holders of territory awakened.

Later that night Boorana finds his way out of the reserve
by a gap in the fence and walks downhill into open country.
He crosses a plowed field and is now in a state of such
confusion that he could well curl up in the usual koala
resting posture and remain so until death ensues. But there
is nothing taller than a fencepost to climb, until he comes
to a relic of the forests that once covered the district—an
aged forest red gum, full of dead limbs and yet with a few
sparse clusters of foliage floating like wispy clouds against
the stars. It is a vastly different-looking tree from those
planted in the Tucki Tucki reserve.

Being a koala, Boorana is soon on his way up. He starts
to feed on a clump of leaves sprouting from the main
trunk, and by dawn he is asleep in the fork of a large
branch and the main stem. Both prongs of the fork itself
are dead, but the timber, though seamed and weathered,
is stout. A dog barking from a nearby farm does not dis-
turb him. He has heard dogs bark before. A heavy truck
roars along the road on the ridge, its headlights yellow in
the misty morning, and from the bushes overhanging a

stream at the bottom of the hill comes the rounded call
of the swamp pheasant.

No other koala is taken from the second-growth forest
on the far side of Gloucester before clearing starts. The
farmer has put his dogs back in their kennels, and Talgara
has returned to her former sleeping place in the pine tree.
This leaves two young males, a mature female with "embryonic" young in pouch, and an old male, somewhere in
the eucalypt scrub about to be cleared. Of these, the mature
female is catapulted into a thicket of wattles soon after
work begins, and the next night the old male sets out in
the quiet of the dark for some other place, any place, the
continuing racket of a day's bulldozing having altogether
upset him. The first is captured and caged by the driver
of the bulldozer, at some cost to himself, as his shirt and
chest are badly ripped when he holds the terrified animal
facing him. The second starts out in the direction of the
gully but, meeting the undergrowth of privet and lantana,
turns north and eventually reaches a stand of spotted gum,
with some stringybarks and ironbarks. Though fairly safe
from disturbance, he is now isolated, and the possibility
of his ever coming into contact with another koala is remote. There are a few eucalypts in groups in the district,
and though travel between them may be somewhat hazardous, the food supply will certainly outlast him, and he will
probably die of old age.

Another koala is captured before the clearing is finished:
the sharp-eyed driver of the bulldozer spots a young male
on a low branch a second or two before he is due to knock

the tree out of the ground. He manages to stop in time. Descending stiffly from his seat, he flexes his leg muscles, wipes the sweat from his eyes, sighs, and prepares to take another prisoner. The last one, he recollects, ripped his shirt to ribbons and treated the skin of his chest in much the same way. But this koala is blind. Hearing footsteps and doubtless scenting the presence of a strange animal, the small creature starts to cry out. The sound is indistinguishable from the crying of a young child. The man touches its fur, and the sound ceases. Then he notices that the koala is very emaciated and that all the leaves within reach have been eaten. So he breaks a spray from another tree, which is eagerly accepted. When it is finished, the koala gropes for more. The driver, who is now near enough to be able to see in greater detail, then notices that the koala's eyes are closed and comes to the conclusion that they have been sealed by the encrustation around them. This in fact is what sometimes happens to victims of a particular disease when, especially in fine sunny weather, the discharge from the eyes dries while the animal is asleep in the daytime and actually produces a state of blindness before the infection has advanced to that stage where the power of sight itself starts to fail.

After supplying more leaves, the rescuer lifts the koala down, finding only tractability and calmness after a moment's concern at being plucked out of its tree. From there the patient is handed over to the farmer's son, to be picked up a few days later by the ranger and taken to Koala Park, near Sydney, for treatment. The mature female with young is released at Port Macquarie, where provision has already been made by the townspeople for a community of koalas within the boundaries of their town.

Except for a thin line of trees to serve as a windbreak, the entire forest of second-growth eucalypts has now been reduced to heaps of wood for burning. In future years the younger trees will do the work now being carried out by the aging pines. For the present, Talgara sleeps in the pines and feeds in the incipient windbreak with the young male who followed her across the harshlands. Of the eight grown koalas who escaped from the fires and the effects of the fires, they are the only two left in that locality.

Both are already showing an amazing tolerance toward the sights and sounds of the farm—voices, the noise of motors, and the barking of dogs.

There is no interruption to the spell of balmy weather, and the first month of winter ends in fine, warm, sunny days and cool, starry nights.

# JULY

It is noon and midwinter, the green hills around Lismore lying at the bottom of an ocean of sunlight. Or it could be said that they are set in amber, since there is no breath of air to sway the grass or to ruffle the trees along the roadsides.

Some more trees have been left to protect the tops of the ridges from erosion; others mark the course of a creek winding toward the North Arm of the Richmond. There are also a few, older and bigger, standing in isolation on cleared slopes that were once covered with forest.

The eucalypts where the three koalas were released are clustered along a hogback and do not extend far down its sides. Though young, they are numerous enough to form a body of foliage so nearly opaque that it appears to be as luxuriant as that of the camphor laurels whose vivid

113

green is in evidence in so many places about the countryside. There are camphor laurels of every size, from seedlings upward, and Boorana has taken refuge in a clump of
fairly big ones growing around a forest red gum. The en-
circled eucalypt is a giant of its kind, but a giant dying of
old age, and its branches rise out of the massed camphor
laurels like the spars of a ship sinking into a shimmering
sea. Only a few tufts of leaves are left, high up on the
last veins of living bark, and it is here the koala has been
feeding.

Boorana has made no journey of his own free choice
since his arrival in the district and, having at last found a
place where he has been left alone, is not likely to move
on while there is a single leaf of his present food supply
remaining. But the moment of its exhaustion is not now
far away. He has always retreated in this direction or in
that—in any direction, in fact, as long as it takes him
away from the hostility of the entrenched males—and
when he is forced once again to go in search of another
food tree the only certainty is that he will not try to re-
trace his steps. Red tag N.P.W.S. 86 M will never again
be recorded in the Tucki Tucki reserve, even though its
wearer is heavier and stronger than any of the landholders
there.

That evening the big koala—big, that is, for that lati-
tude—wakes at sunset and climbs up a branch of the forest
red gum, his rounded form conspicuous against the clouded
sky. It is raining to the south, but the last light of day
shows up the nearer terrain clearly. A short distance away
is the timbered ridge of the reserve, the road up to it dotted

with trees, as is the road down to the Tuckean Swamp,
where the olivine foliage of some scattered eucalypts overtops the brighter green of camphor laurels. Casuarinas in
and around the swamp flow darkly across the flats, and
two forest red gums stand against the sky like gigantic
black bushes. Both of these are alive, but their foliage is
so thin that the design and spread of each branch is plain.
Recently Boorana spent a day and a night in them, only
to be put to flight by—incredibly—the mere grumblings
of a male koala on his way back to his own territory.

Besides the koalas in the reserve, there are others in some
of the pockets of eucalypts thereabouts—near the Tuckean
Swamp, in forest red gums near a church, in the grounds
of a school, in trees along the road, at Tuckurimba, at
Broadwater, at Riley's Hill and Rous Mill, and in other
places no doubt kept secret by people who know and fear
the interest of those who might interfere with the best of
intentions and the worst of results.

Formerly the district supported a great number of koalas,
but the tide of eucalypts is ebbing, and it is only where
a few food trees remain that any of these quaint little
marsupials may now be found. Nevertheless, even if their
near-extermination is a tragedy, the survival of some of them
in certain closely settled areas is a miracle, for it is almost
unbelievable that creatures of specialized diet, fitted only
for an arboreal existence, should have the toughness to
subsist in the odds and ends of habitat left to them. Indeed, so discontinuous are the remaining scraps that they
can hardly be called a habitat at all—any more than a grassy
patch surrounded by dogs, roads, automobiles, and houses

could be called a habitat for, say, four or five kangaroos.

However, that contradictory animal the koala seems to have a genius for ignoring every other species, distraction, and danger outside a radius of ten meters and, if left alone, seems able to live wherever the climate is mild and there is a supply of food.

Boorana finishes the rest of the leaves on the forest red gum and descends into the camphor laurels. Light rain is falling. The camphor laurels shiver in a breeze and shed water constantly. The koala pauses awhile to break off some of their leaves and, after smelling them, eats one or two. The rest fall from his paws as he continues his descent. Having reached the ground, he picks his way through long paspalum grass with evident dislike for its depth and density. He crosses the road but, finding the paspalum just as high and thick on the other side, returns to the paved surface. Most wild creatures would have shown some trepidation, or at least curiosity, at encountering such a different feature of their environment, but to the koala a road is just a place for easy walking. It is fortunate for Boorana that no vehicle of any kind comes along at that particular time, as the rain on the asphalt and the reflections always supplied by approaching headlights, together with his dark-drenched fur, would have made him very difficult to see.

Boorana knows where he is going. He has been there before but left in response to a threat from a koala in a nearby tree. He is now a cowed and timid fugitive in a strange environment which, soured as it is with the hostility of other males, has become an obstacle too formidable to be surmounted. He is making for a tallowwood in the corner of a horse paddock. Sometimes other koalas pass along that way but seldom visit the tallowwood, which is aside from the natural travel lines between one feeding ground and the next. Taking a track up a low cutting, Boorana skirts a fence and crosses a garden with all the nonchalance of a household pet, again demonstrating the fact that his fearfulness stops short of most things outside his experience as a wild creature.

Being now very close to his goal, he breaks into a canter and climbs swiftly into the stubby branches of the lopped tallowwood. Such make-do refuges are the lot of the outcast.

Neither of the two females freed with him has suffered any hostility anywhere, the elder—the female with empouched young—not having moved farther than a hundred meters from where she was released. Food trees are plentiful in the reserve, and she has no difficulty in always having one to herself; and although her present surroundings are different from any others she has known, they are also kinder and have made her transfer so easy that she shows no trace of restlessness. Similarly, the young female is entirely untroubled, though she remains as likely as ever to wander away at any time and into any kind of country. Indeed, on the same night that Boorana becomes stranded in the lone tallowwood, the sixteen-month-old female tagged N.P.W.S. 88F crosses the road from the Tucki Tucki reserve and, after cutting across the short grass of a paddock where cattle have been grazing, climbs into a forest red gum on the side of the road leading down to

the Tuckean Swamp. That night she feeds in the eucalypt
—one of the few in the vicinity—and sleeps there the
following day.

The next night she passes more camphor laurels and
casuarinas, and then swings from the upper branches of
a swamp turpentine, where she has fed briefly, into a
sapling eucalypt which bends so flexibly under her weight
that she is obliged to swivel quickly around to keep her
head uppermost and avoid the risk of sliding off. And
there she hangs, like a giant fruit bat or a large nocturnal
bird, eating steadily. The branchlet is so slim that she finds
difficulty in clinging on, and finally the end leaves strip
away and she falls into the paspalum grass.

Two wildlife rangers completing a count of the koalas
in the district do not notice N.P.W.S. 88F asleep in the
casuarinas when they drive by in the morning. As their
search must be completed that day, they have no opportunity of making a recount, and in any case, when they
are sitting in an open timber shelter in the reserve, check-
ing and amplifying their notes late the same afternoon,
they find the results of their survey to be much as they
would have forecast.

It is always better to make a rough count of koalas in
an area, even a snap count as this one is, before doing any
catching—that is, if an idea of distribution as well as
numbers is required—because koalas taken in the wild
state always scatter in alarm as soon as they are put back
in the trees. The exodus, which begins when the first captives are released—and they should be released promptly
—causes a population vacuum in one locality and an arti-

ficial build-up of numbers in others, and it may take as long as a month for the "natural" pattern to re-form.

The count just completed has been necessarily hurried because a biologist from the National Parks and Wildlife Service and a microbiologist from the District Veterinary Laboratory of the Department of Agriculture at Armidale are due next day to examine and take blood samples from every koala in the reserve. They hope to finish the work in two days. The biologist from the head office of the N.P.W.S. in Sydney is studying population dynamics— birthrate, aging, growth and development, and mortality— feeding preferences, movement, and general behavior, while the microbiologist from Armidale requires further blood samples and eye swabs to continue his study of an eye disease prevalent among koalas. This particular infection causes a severe inflammation of the cornea and the conjunctiva, leading to progressive blindness. It is thought that recovery is rare, as the blind koalas apparently lose confidence in tree-climbing and thus find it increasingly difficult to forage and ultimately die from starvation. Affected koalas are often found dead at the base of eucalyptus trees.

One of the two rangers making the preliminary count returns to his own region that evening, while the other loads his station wagon with catching gear for the morning. That night it rains.

There is a small shelter shed at Tucki Tucki. It has a low table, rustic style, surrounded by a rectangle of logs as seats. The shed is open on three sides, and the occasional gust of wind does not trouble itself to go around.

The morning is dark, and the light will not improve. Rain is belting on the roof as on a drum and spraying off the stone-paved apron outside from the force of impact. The spray is a bright ground fog. Peter Moore, the microbiologist, hunched up with concentration, is arranging hypodermic needles and glass phials for blood samples. He puts a bottle of pure alcohol on the table and tips some balls of cotton into a cardboard box. Trevor Breen, the biologist from the National Parks and Wildlife Service, is a man knowledgeable in the ways of the koala. He is also very tall and has already bumped his head twice on exactly the same place on the overhang of the shelter shed. He does not comment on the quaintness of this coincidence—or, if he does, his words are lost in the roar of rain on the roof. Having arranged his forms and other sheets of paper in plastic envelopes to protect them from the fine mist of spray drifting through the shed, he assists Peter Moore with his preparations.

Outside, Max Prentice, the wildlife ranger for the area, is setting a light aluminum extension ladder against a tallowwood. Wan glints of light ripple over his black weather gear, filmed as it is with running water. When he looks up, he has to shield his eyes against the heavy raindrops spinning down and expanding against the wind-blown trees as they fall. Even so, they sting him sometimes.

Max has brought a rope ladder too, in case it should be needed. There are three canvas bags besides, and two aluminum poles, each with a piece of burlap attached to an end. One of the poles is five meters long, the other three and a half. Some coils of rope and a long nylon cord complete the equipment. A quick check, and he goes into the shelter shed and removes his dripping sou'wester. He is older than either of the other two, with short graying hair and the carriage of a high-ranking ex-soldier.

"Ready?"

Peter nods in a preoccupied manner, moves a glass phial three millimeters to the left, then back, and says, "Yes."

Trevor Breen hurriedly lashes some clock-faced scales to a rafter, Max replaces his sou'wester, and the sound of rain on the roof turns to a steady pattering on the waterproofs on the three men.

Although none of the trees in the reserve could be called a veteran, the tallowwood the ladder is leaning against is a full twenty-five meters high, and the koala Max has spotted is in its topmost plume of foliage.

Peter is the tree-climber; a young man and muscular, alert to the dangers of rotten stubs and only occasionally inclined to take risks, he continues his ascent from the top of the ladder by a series of conveniently placed branches, then, finding the main stem slimmer than he had thought, calls for the longer of the two poles. It is taken up by Trevor and handed from the top of the ladder. Thrusting it through the high foliage, Peter waves it over the koala's head. It is hard, muscle-wrenching work, for the burlap is now drenched and the wind is strong.

Whether the koala fears the waving material simply because of its size and the swishing noise it makes among the leaves, or because it gives the impression of an attack by a wedge-tailed eagle, which may well be a natural hazard for the species, there is no doubt about the effectiveness of this method of forcing the quarry to come down.

However, descent continues only as far as the first fork, where it turns into an ascent of the other prong. The burlap swoops, and the koala backs away again, then, as the folds settle momentarily around her, jumps to a lower branch, which gives so flexibly that she is soon hanging by her forelegs. She drops to a cluster of leaves underneath, and when that swings down under her weight, she is less than five meters from the ground, with no chance of climbing up again, at least not while the burlap is hovering above.

"She'll grab the next lot of leaves, so keep her coming," Trevor calls.

So the burlap swirls again, and the koala, obviously badly frightened, tumbles onto the next lower bunch of foliage, immediately slithers off, and falls to the ground. She lands on her belly and is running before Max can reach her. But he soon overtakes her and, holding her by the neck and loins, presses her gently but firmly into the grass. To lift her now, without a better grip, would be to set her claws clutching at anything within range, so he waits. She starts to squeal and growl. She is a cleanskin—no tag in her ear—and has never been handled before. Trevor stands by with an opened canvas bag as her captor takes a new grip of the scruff of her neck and, putting his other hand under her rump, lifts her, her legs spread like a crab's, and tosses her backward into the bag.

The next koala is taken in a forest red gum, and he does have a tag in his ear. He is very young, having been caught

and tagged only four months ago. He is so young he makes
not the slightest attempt to escape, not even when Trevor
Breen lifts him out from among the leaves and descends
the ladder with the prisoner pressed against his waterproof
coat. There is a half-eaten leaf projecting from the young
koala's mouth, and he starts munching again just before
he plunges backward into the second of the canvas bags.

An old male koala in the northeast corner of the reserve
is picked out to occupy the last of the three bags, but he
is warier than the others and crosses into another tree
before Peter can get near him. So the rope ladder and
the long pole are thrown down again, and, Peter having
descended, the extension ladder is placed against the
adjacent tree. Whereupon the koala swings back to where
he was before and moves out to the end of a lateral.

Seeing a chance to cut him off, the men return the
ladder to its former position, and the climber swarms up,
followed by Trevor Breen with the aluminum pole. As
the koala tries to repeat his former stratagem, a wildly
flapping object arises out of the leaves to bar his way. He
retreats. But he does not descend. Now that the initial
shock has passed, he does not seem to be unduly alarmed
and keeps threatening the burlap with one or the other
of his front paws, his talons dangerously spread.

Then Peter, who has been lying along a wet and slippery
branch, revolves suddenly and accidentally to its underside, and the burlap flops into the leaves beside the koala,
who immediately strikes at it, entangling a front paw. The
man, re-established, hauls on the pole. The koala grunts
and roars as his arm is pulled out straight. But he has a

good grip with three of his four paws, and Peter's fiercest tug fails to dislodge him.

"Go easy," Max yells from down below. "You'll pull his arm off."

A fizz of amusement explodes from Peter's compressed lips. "You mean he'll pull mine off. Anyway"—he rests—"never move him this way."

"Chuck up the noose," Trevor calls, and Max throws it neatly. It is passed on, but now Peter cannot drag the pole free. Knowing that the burlap is tied on with only a single strand, he keeps on jagging until it chafes through and the burlap is left dangling. Then a stiffened nylon loop on the end of the pole is gently pushed toward the koala, who makes no attempt to dodge. The man draws it tight around the animal's neck. The nylon cord has the quality of loosening as soon as the strain is off, and this is just as well, for trying to shift the koala by pulling on a cord is as hopeless as trying by pulling on a pole—more so. Now the koala has a grip with four paws. His roarings, squealings, and gruntings become steadily hoarser as the cord constricts his breathing. But he does not budge.

Peter slackens off. "Never get him this way either," he says.

He drops the end of the cord to Max, whose experimental tugging from the ground immediately terrifies the koala by threatening to twist him into the head-down position, which would nullify the set of his talons. The quarry's guttural uproar is now interspersed with incongruous squealing cries, but, though partly dislodged, he manages to pivot around so that his head is again uppermost. He continues to slip slowly down the sheaf of leaves he is clutching. Suddenly the cord is swinging loose in the wind.

"He'll be killed from that height," Max objects. "Take a turn around that branch out to the side."

The cord bellies toward Peter, who has descended from the treetop by this time. Grabbing it at the third attempt, he passes it over a whippy branch above his head and begins to haul, and now the direction of the strain is widely angled. However, it is still downward, though by no means directly so, and, with nothing to grasp except the leaves already bunched in his "arms," the koala falls. But he does not fall far before Peter, showing a nice judgment and aided by the resilience of the branch overhead, brakes the speed of the drop without any semblance of a jerk and holds the koala dangling. He lowers away until the captive's rear feet touch. Fighting mad, the koala spins about with both forelegs open, ready to clutch or strike. There is no sign of fear about him now. He is in a towering rage. Securing him is a scuffling affair, but finally the last of the black talons are enveloped and the neck of the bag is tied.

They carry the catch back to the shelter and decide to deal with the young koala first. So he is permitted to walk part way out of the bag, which is then gathered around his neck. He looks absurdly like a dwarf about to have a haircut. Max holds him in a sitting position on his knees while Trevor measures the head from its occipital crest to the base of the nose, then to the end of the nose. The youngster's mouth is prized open with a twig and the state of his teeth noted. He is reckoned to be seventeen months old. The state of his fur provokes comment. It appears to be quite dry, though he was taken in pouring rain and dumped into a saturated canvas bag. Certainly his fur is fluffy. One after another, the men stroke his head with their fingertips. There is no trace of water. His skin, too, seems to be dry.

Max pulls a fold of the canvas over the koala's head and produces a furry right foreleg. It is inert, the small black talons half curled. Peters clips away a patch of fur on the "forearm," dabs with alcohol, and pricks the cephalic vein with a hypodermic needle. After taking a small blood sample, he squirts it into a phial, which he labels with the number that is on the koala's ear tag.

At the conclusion of a quick all-over examination, the absence of external parasites is noted and the subject is weighed while suspended from a cord looped around the body and under the forelegs. All this proceeds in silence as far as the koala is concerned, even when he is slowly gyrating from the scales. His weight: 3.30 kilograms. They return him to the bag in order to release him later in the same tree from which he was taken.

Except for an occasional brief bout of struggling and squealing, the female is processed without any trouble and, being a newcomer to the reserve, is given an ear tag. She is well past middle age, her molars and pre-molars being worn down to a common flatness almost at gum level. She is at least seven, perhaps eight. The young one in her pouch is attached to the teat. Taking a measurement as best he can through the pouch's furry skin, Trevor estimates the young koala to be about five months old.

It is lying in the usual position, across the dorsal line and above the pouch's opening. The mother's weight is 5.80 kilograms, and her fur, like that of the young male koala, is dry.

Then it is the old male's turn, and he roars and grunts and fights from first to last. He grumbles while his head is measured, seizes the stick between his powerful rear molars and chews it to splinters when Trevor Breen tries to look at his teeth, and never fails to snap at any hand that may come near his mouth. His long, rodentlike lower incisors can inflict a painful bite, though it is not to be compared in severity with a slicing scratch from his front talons. He is silent for a short time while his head is smothered in the canvas bag and his foreleg produced for Peter to take a blood sample, but the prick of the needle sets him off again, and Max, temporarily hard put to it to hold him, has constant thoughts of being bitten through the bag. However, the really big performance comes when the koala is being weighed. All legs flailing, he jerks about so furiously that it is minutes before the indicator on the clock face can be read. He weighs 8.5 kilograms. And he makes enough noise for a herd of pigs. Finally he is bagged again and taken away with the other two to be released.

The work goes on all day, and it rains all day. By three in the afternoon there is a new creek running along a grassy hollow to the east. The sky starts to clear at sunset.

Twenty-two koalas are caught in and around the reserve that day, and seventeen the next day in fine weather, making a total of thirty-nine—enough to yield a lot of information.

And the first item of information, at least for those not acquainted with the ways of the koala, is the fact that so many animals were caught in less than two days by the direct method of pursuit. It is no reflection on the skill of the catchers to say that most other arboreal creatures would have had to be trapped. But the koala, besides having a fixed idea that the branch of a tree is a place safe from every enemy, is a slow mover and lacking in agility when compared with possums and gliders.

Time after time, the inability of the koala to descend speedily was demonstrated; and whenever one tried to escape by jumping to another branch, the actual jump was always more of a lunge than a leap, with never any impression of that sailing through space which so often occurs when the performer is assisted both in achievement and in grace by a long and flowing tail.

In fact, after watching a number of such jumps the observer is left with the feeling that if a koala were to attempt anything really spectacular it might well start revolving head over heels in midair and so put its talons and the great strength of its limbs to their severest test—but a test that would almost certainly be passed, for it is in gripping power alone that the koala can outdo most other tree-dwellers.

Of the thirty-nine koalas caught, eighteen were mature females, all except three with empouched young. The ages of the young ones ranged in general from about four and a half months to seven months—though in one case the "embryonic" young was not more than three months. There was a marked scarcity of two- and three-year-olds, a disclosure that Trevor Breen said had special significance because it tied in with the known history of the members of this age group. Blind wanderings about a district where a former abundance of food trees no longer obtains can well prove to be disastrous.

All the established males living in the reserve were located in their own territories, except one, and he has probably gone a-roving for a few days but will be back in his usual place when the next check is made in two months' time. This habit of taking a short leave seems to be pretty general among old males and is quite dissimilar from the journeyings of the young, since the older animals are never lost and always return to their starting point.

As for the mature females, these were, without exception, still in the area and, again without exception, distributed at random throughout the various male territories. The full-grown female member of the last group of three released in the reserve, N.P.W.S. 87F, has moved only to the other side of the ridge, but the young female tagged N.P.W.S. 88F was not sighted. While not discounting the possibility that she may have met with a predator— she is little more than a cub—the rangers are more inclined to believe she has simply behaved true to type by wandering aimlessly about the district.

The old male, N.W.P.S. 86M, has also disappeared—a development not a bit surprising to men aware of the forces operating against the successful transference of any mature male koala to country already occupied by other males. Boorana, the rangers correctly assume, is on the run; and if his red tag is ever seen again, it will probably be accompanied by a note saying it was taken from a dead animal. But the site of his death could be revealing. As the men sit there, intent upon their noting and their reasoning, the dappled patterns of leaf and branch swaying back and forth upon the ground give way gradually to the barred shadows of tree trunks which do not move, except to lengthen toward the deep, reflective blue of the eastern sky. A cool winter's breeze stirs the eucalypts, and a male koala in the top of a tallowwood in a corner of the reserve suddenly starts uttering a gruff, regular cry. He sounds as though he is snoring. Perhaps he is. He is always there. At least he has been there every day for weeks and is known to many a passer-by. He is very old, very obese, very sluggish and quits the tallowwood's crest for some neighboring eucalypt only occasionally, for a brief change of diet.

As the men gather up their gear and walk toward their station wagon outside the dogproof fence, a party of currawongs crosses the valley, rising and falling as though tossed by invisible waves. Although the birds are a long way off, they are easily identified by their flight pattern and method—having neither—and by the loud, ringing calls that come floating on the breeze, calls seeming to have that strange raffish quality inseparable from currawongs everywhere. One by one, like black feather dusters, they fall out of the sky and plunge into a sea of light green foliage.

"When do the camphor laurels fruit?" Peter murmurs, nodding in the direction of the source of another round of bold hulloos and lilting whistles.

"All the year round, if you ask me," is the reply.

As they turn the station wagon toward Lismore, they see the currawongs on the next leg of their journey to their roosting places, dipping and soaring, high, wide, and handsome, in the general direction of some trees growing along a creek.

Because of their habit of regurgitating the hard skins and seeds of the fruit they eat and digesting only the pulpy parts, the big black-and-white birds are very effective distributors of many kinds of plants, including the intro-duced camphor laurel and privet. Beneath almost every obvious perching place in the region there is a concentra-tion of camphor laurel seedlings or saplings, which has certainly sprung from pellets disgorged by currawongs; and there does seem to be a danger that the wide-spreading exotics will gradually crowd out most of the native trees now growing along roadsides and in the parks and reserves of the north coast of New South Wales. The wildlife rangers, however, realizing that the seed-carriers are as Australian as the displaced eucalypts, believe that the camphor laurel's exuberance should be controlled—if it is to be controlled—by methods not detrimental to any of their charges.

Boorana leaves the tallowwood after a few days and walks to a grove of casuarinas and paperbarks in a hollow at the bottom of the horse paddock. Despite the cold weather, myriads of mosquitoes have bred in floodwater left by the heavy rain, and the koala quickly becomes the object of their attacks. He smells the leaves of the paper-bark but does not eat.

Outside, in the open air, the stars are bright, and the

breeze from the south sways the massed foliage of the swamp-loving trees, soughing through the broomlike tufts of the casuarina stalks and rustling the paperbarks. Sometimes a glint of light shines from a stagnant pool lying among the roots of the trees where no breath of air can reach. The mosquitoes swarm around Boorana, stinging his eyes, nose, and ears so viciously that he is soon on the move again.

He and the young female N.P.W.S. 88F are on opposite sides of the Tuckean Swamp at this time. Boorana returns to the road, where he finds an isolated gray gum; she makes her way across open country and is picked up eventually, bedraggled and hungry, by a farm worker. Her rescuer, on his way from Rous Mill to Woodburn, leaves her in a small reserve at Broadwater, about twelve kilometers from where he found her, but never does get around to informing the right people of the markings on her ear tag. As soon as she is full-fed she wanders off again, as casually as though she were surrounded by untouched forests of eucalypts instead of cultivated lands where food trees are almost nonexistent. She is so absolutely unaffected by her recent experiences, slight as they may be, that her chances of reaching maturity must be rated as poor.

Some hundreds of kilometers south, on the morning of the day the yearling female left the Broadwater reserve on another stage of her aimless journeyings, the early sun is golden on the east side of the pine tree where Talgara is asleep. Her cub has grown considerably in the last two or three weeks and is now a fully furred, solidly built koala nearly eighteen centimeters long and, as no part of this

measurement is taken up by a tail, a fairly bulky passenger
for an animal the size of Talgara. He has at last relin-
quished his grip of the teat that has kept him anchored
since his initial attachment a few minutes after his birth
nearly seven months ago. As a consequence, he is now
able to move about freely within the pouch. Like his
mother, he sleeps a lot, and, also like his mother, he seems
to lack curiosity. Although he has peered out now and
then, he has seen nothing but a grayish mist of fur, his
mother being at rest on each occasion.

Of the daytime life of the outside world Talgara knows
little more than the diurnal animals know of the world of
darkness. She will never see, for instance, the lorikeets
flying down the sky to feed in the flowering eucalypts as
they have done every morning for the past ten days. They
are there now, their voices shrill in the frosty air, and the
light flashes on their wings as they settle in the treetops
and then whirl up again to mingle, screaming, with the
myriads of other nomads—rainbows, musks, and scaly-
breasted green-and-golds—pouring in from way beyond
towns and farming lands to where the great trees stand
in a deep and unchanged gully, to tallowwoods dripping
with nectar and to the scents of winter blossoms in the
sunshine. It is blossoming time for the flooded gums, too,
and though they are not as generous in their flow of honey
as the tallowwoods, they are so rich in pollen that there
are as many lorikeets swinging from their flower heads as
there are in the tallowwoods.

The wreckage of the bulldozed area of second-growth
forest between the edge of the gully and the house is now,

of course, a disaster zone for most of the defenseless creatures living there and, for the same reason, a happy hunting ground for kookaburras, butcher birds, and magpies.

Concealed in the thin line of eucalypts that has been preserved to take the place eventually of the aging pine trees, a butcher bird watches the clearing for signs of movement on the churned-up ground and for small birds attempting the perilous crossing. A magpie planes smoothly down to join his companions on the ground, his black-and-white wings motionless until they suddenly beat once, twice, and fold as he stalls and alights in the same instant. With his beak pointing intently down, a kookaburra waits for the warming sunshine to set the lizards running in fits and starts among the debris of piled branches, and for some of them perhaps to venture into the open.

The lorikeets leave the big trees in the gully well before sunset, the butcher birds and magpies go when it is dusk, and later, soon after dark, just as the day's last wild requiem of kookaburra laughter is ringing out, Talgara descends from her pine tree. Her climbing position is awkward and must be difficult to maintain, as she is holding her body clear of the tree to preserve her bulky cub—and her pouch—from being bumped and scraped against the trunk. The eucalypts seem very close to the ground after the height of the pine tree, and there is only one forest red gum among them. Even this is eaten out, as is a tallowwood. Most of the other trees in the incipient windbreak are blackbutts and, though Talgara spent many days in the gully asleep in a blackbutt, she seldom ate of its foliage and then sparingly.

That night the farmer and his son let the dogs off their chains to prevent the koalas' return to the pine trees. The plan works, and Talgara and the young male are easily detected in the eucalypts next day and captured by the same methods as those used earlier by the ranger.

The reasons for this sudden development are well-meaning and spring from a desire to save the koalas from slow starvation by presenting them to a man and his wife who have assured the farmer that they have just moved into a suburb of Sydney where there are already "hundreds of koalas."

So the same afternoon, at the end of a six-hour journey on the rear seat of a car, two corn bags are opened in a garden on the Barrenjoey Peninsula. The garden is large enough to contain some wide-spreading rusty gums, and, quite unaware of the illegality of their act in taking protected animals, the poorly informed saviors watch the koalas climb for the higher branches. Because of the trees' open habit and lightness of foliage, both animals are gratifyingly easy to see—but what the owners of the property do not know is that "rusty gum" and "red gum" are merely popular names for the smooth-barked apple or angophora, a non-eucalypt koalas do not eat from preference.

Neither of the new arrivals is there in the morning. Already acquainted with the sounds of voices, motors, and the barking of dogs, and having suffered little effect from their brief imprisonment, they backed down from their respective trees soon after the darkness had become comparatively quiet. The young male moved into a gray gum in a nearby garden, but Talgara went the opposite way. The following night she wanders farther in the same direction, across lawns and flowerbeds and along gravel paths, completely failing to see, on one occasion, a big dog lying on a veranda. Nor does she notice him suddenly look up and remain at gaze while she passes, nor hear the *clop* of jaws as his heavy head bumps down again onto the veranda's tiled surface. He exhales gustily and closes his eyes. Trained from puppyhood not to attack other animals, and having been especially schooled to ignore the koalas that sometimes amble through the grounds, the dog is the first proof of the influence of the Avalon Preservation Trust and other similar bodies whose members are mostly drawn from the locality.

Briefly conspicuous in the light of a street lamp, Talgara climbs into a eucalypt of a kind new to her, a swamp mahogany.

# AUGUST

At the start of the third month of winter, the blind koala originally rescued by the bulldozer driver is eating the leaves of a forest red gum in a warmed, glass-enclosed room at Koala Park. He is in isolation, and this seems to suit him.

His eyes were first bathed open and have now been restored to normal by the use of an antibiotic ointment recently found to give good results in the treatment of the disease. Both the speed of recovery and the absence of shock are probably due to the youth of the subject.

But a question has arisen concerning his release. The National Parks and Wildlife Service is not anxious to have him liberated in a reserve or in the bush, in case the disease should appear again and infect other koalas; and, even if permission were given by the authorities for the inclusion of another protected animal among those already at Koala Park, the owner is not prepared to run the risk of the possible infection of his own koalas.

As soon as final arrangements have been made for the setting aside of a suitable island, perhaps in Myall Lakes on the midcoast of New South Wales, for the reception of koalas who have suffered from eye disease, not only will the problem of relocation be solved but also it will be possible to find out whether in fact the condition can recur. So for the time being the captive must wait in his comfortable prison.

Only a few kilometers from this scene, the breeze off Pittwater is rustling the large pendent leaves of a swamp mahogany. The sun is in the west, and the camphor laurels and weeping willows across the flats are an opaque green barrier behind a filigree of light-filled eucalypts. There are lawns and houses among the trees, and long shadows on the grass. A crimson rosella, brilliant in the sunshine, flashes through the branches of the eucalypts and vanishes over the tops of the camphor laurels in the background.

No main road comes near the flatland, but the noise of engines is always audible, sometimes in the distance, sometimes close by. Talgara has slept throughout the day in the swamp mahogany, apparently undisturbed by voices and the clinking of wrenches as two boys work on a motor boat. But when the engine blasts suddenly into life the koala is so violently shocked that both her forelegs flick out straight at shoulder height. An arrow of foam whitens the sparkling blue of the inlet and is abruptly quenched in the shadow of the western ridge. Talgara settles again into rotundity, peers rather vaguely around, then folds her arms and bends her head. Now every sound is a faraway sound, except the lapping of wavelets on the stones of the retaining wall.

But she does not sleep long, and as she stands up her cub burrows into her pouch, leaving only a hind foot in view. He is now seven months old and ventures out occasionally when his parent is at rest. Talgara climbs higher in the stiff-legged manner made necessary by the size of her burden and its awkward placing. She has accepted the swamp mahogany as a food tree and after two days' feeding shows no inclination to change to another kind of eucalypt.

When she does move away, she goes to a gray gum on the curve of the road on the other side of the park and exactly where every car coming from the direction of Newport flashes its headlights through the foliage as it bounces out of a hollow, with the result that every now and then Talgara is startled into momentary immobility by a soundless explosion of light among the branches. She descends as soon as the neighborhood is quiet, and walks down the middle of the road.

As she passes directly under each street lamp, she changes from a dark moving shape into a koala the color of mist. She walks under the turnstile of a children's playground and tries to climb a hardwood fence but can get no grip on its dense, oiled surface. For a while she bobs up and down, making loud raspings with her front claws and only once clearing the ground with all four feet—and then but for an instant. So she follows the fence along two sides of a square and returns to the street. After going through the first open gate, she crosses a garden, then other gardens, few of the houses having fences, and walks into another park, or reserve, which is partly submerged by a mass of lantana. She finds a path that is half tunnel. There are the scents of other koalas. She follows the path.

She follows it only as far as another gray gum, which she climbs. But the gray gum is eaten out, as also are others nearby, all having been consistently overbrowsed, and she further endangers the life of every one of them she visits by breaking off any long twigs carrying tufts of leaves that would otherwise have remained out of reach. At length hunger drives her to feed in a spotted gum, and it is dawn when she returns to the ground and almost immediately starts to climb again.

The tree she has now selected, an angophora, easily overtops every other tree in the reserve; and yet, in spite of this, it is really a gigantic misshapen dwarf, so covered with lumps and unexpected oddnesses that its height becomes a secondary characteristic. Some of its great roots have swelled up out of the soil and gleam faintly in the early daylight, while others, doubtless, dive deep to offset the pull of branches that swoop and curve and recurve and sprout knobs like the stumps of amputated limbs and spread out so far that it seems miraculous they do not fall in ruins and split the column of the main trunk down.

Though ascent is slow, the koala rises steadily into the brightening sky and is invisible from the ground by the

time the sun starts to paint in the pastel pinks and grays
and blues and purples of the tree's prodigious woody
growth and traces out its convolutions. The mark where
two branches have met and fused is plain. It is a tree of
delicate and changing tones, of grotesque shapes and
masses, and it is full of light.

With her liking for sleeping far out on a lateral, Talgara takes a little while to settle down. There are no whippy
horizontal wands on an angophora. So she stays on the
platform of a branch's junction with the main trunk and
does not stir until late in the afternoon. Her cub does not
attempt to get into her pouch but clings to her frontal
fur instead, a position less inconvenient for the climber
than being in the pouch. In any case, the latter position
is now impossible because of the size of the young one.
In spite of his rapid growth, however, he is but skimpily
covered and not yet in the proper form of a koala, lacking
the roundness and fluffiness he will have in, say, another
month. Furthermore, his head has not quite lost the elongated and rectangular lines which added to the freakish
appearance of the "embryonic" mite.

Talgara eats some of the leaves of the angophora, but
her offspring, though he takes some in his paws, finally
rejects them. When she descends that night, he remains
in the underslung position, and it is almost another week
before she pushes him onto her back. There is no doubt
as to his state when this further development takes place,
and it is one of abject fear. His head is pressed so closely
against his parent's body that he is not able to see the

lights of the suburb shining from outside the boundaries of the reserve. But his cries become more piercing as he looks over Talgara's shoulder just as the moon sails magnificently into the clear to reveal the lower branches of the angophora shining as smooth as glass against the dim remoteness of the ground.

Not until the cub is peering out at the world from between his mother's rounded and tufted ears do his protests abate, and down in the street below, a woman who has been standing beside her car gets in and slams the door, having come relievedly to the conclusion that she could not possibly have been listening to a child crying. Probably some kind of animal calling to its mate. She knows there are possums in the reserve.

Although her burden is now situated in the best place for carrying, Talgara does not begin her descent at once. When eventually she backs over the junction of the great branch with the angophora's trunk, she looks down over her shoulder, and her limbs are spread-eagled, her body pressed flat against the bark. To watch her now is to wonder how she got safely down before with the encumbrance of a well-grown cub clinging to her chest or in her pouch. Weird, flickering shapes race through the dark bush as a car's headlights sweep around the corner of an adjacent street. The koala's talons bite deep into the soft outer bark of the angophora.

They are no casual affairs, these journeys down the vertical wall of the huge trunk, yet the cub is now quite at ease, so swiftly do wild creatures come to accept the ordained patterns of their lives. He is sunk so deep in fur and he is so small and so nearly the same shade of gray as his parent that he is practically invisible except for the black sparks which are his eyes.

Talgara goes on down, one backward step after another. Sometimes the talons of one foot slide briefly on the bark before their points catch, but there are always three other sets firmly clamped. Any attempt to slither down, as might happen in the case of a slimmer tree, is out of the question in these circumstances and would certainly end in disaster.

She pauses about four meters above ground and peers around in her myopic manner, listening to the barking of a dog in a house bordering the reserve. The barking stops, and the koala descends the rest of the way. She walks through lantana deep enough to choke out the toughest seedling eucalypt and passes under privet bushes likewise thriving in the rich, moist soil. When she comes to a road she unhesitatingly walks along it. She is a strange sight, this little animal from the back country, and each slick suburban light makes sport of her by sending a shadow to creep after her like a big black cat, then glide past and fade gradually into nothingness.

But she is no more aware of this phenomenon than she is disconcerted later by the glare from a car following at snail's pace, though she does stop once to nose at the road. Turning aside, she climbs a lone scribbly gum with a quick cantering action and starts to feed. Leaves keep brushing across the mouth of the cub, but he is some hours away from having enough confidence to release the grip of a front paw for the instant needed to seize some for himself. However, he manages to catch a leaf in his mouth and, tugging it free, starts to chew.

Talgara never returns to the angophora; neither does she remain in the scribbly gum but transfers from it to another eucalypt, a bangalay. Though her cub still suckles, he has given up his attempts to return to the pouch. His appetite for leaves is steadily increasing.

There are houses to right and left of the tree now sheltering Talgara and her cub; there are jetties too, though none of these things has significance for either of them. Odors bring them more information than do sights or sounds, especially when the breeze is in the north or the northwest and thus free of the puzzling smells of the suburbs.

Occasionally moving about the bangalay during the day, Talgara is inevitably noticed, first by a boy fishing from the retaining wall. He immediately passes on the news of his discovery to the householder, who telephones to the Avalon Preservation Trust, where the presence of a female koala with a young one on her back is noted, together with the date and location. The sighting is marked on a map of the district.

The young male koala caught at the same time as Talgara and later released with her in a nearby garden has also come under observation. He has not traveled far since he ceased to trail after her, and the cross on the map marking his daytime quarters is only a few streets away from where Talgara is at present situated. In point of fact, he is under closer surveillance than she, as his chosen sleeping place is actually in the garden of a member of the Trust especially interested in the movements of koalas in the area and their numbers in relation to the supply of food available.

Accordingly, when he is attacked and slashed by a dog, his plight is soon known to the people best able to help. It is not yet fully light when a sound few Australians have heard and fewer would recognize rises above the soughing of the wind in the trees and around the housetops. It is the unearthly, braying distress call of a koala, and it goes on and on, strengthening and fading and strengthening again in rhythm with the breathing of the victim. The beam from a flashlight reveals the koala squatting on his haunches along the line of a branch, with both front legs rigidly straight, their claws clamped deeply into the bark, and with his mouth wide open. Suddenly the sound stops, and the young koala turns partly away from the watcher to reveal a slit in his skin above the lower back. The dog must have caught him just as he sprang onto the base of the tree, and the wound has bled sufficiently to soak the fur below it.

The first observer gets help from a younger man, and a ladder is procured. Although the koala has by now assumed the position of sleep—or of shock—he is sufficiently perceptive to rouse at the slight impact of the ladder being placed against the tree. Looking up, the man mounting the ladder is surprised to find himself the object of a curious, somewhat sleepy regard.

Having had sufficent experience of wild creatures to know that their expressions do not necessarily correspond with those of human beings, and also having been severely scratched on former occasions, the rescuer pauses to think for a moment but comes quickly to the conclusion that to trust the docile appearance of this small creature would not be nearly so rash as putting his faith in the doggy friendliness of a dingo's grin or accepting at face value the benevolent expression of an estuarine crocodile; and so he reaches up and lifts the koala out of the tree. There is no protest other than the brief clinging of a hind foot to the branch.

As treatment must be somewhat protracted, the veterinarian at Newport, whose services are permanently on offer to the Trust, suggests that the authorities at Taronga Park Zoo be asked to accept the patient. In this way the difficulties of special feeding and warmed quarters with temperature control can be solved. It is not yet midday when the young male koala is in the hands of the zoo's veterinarian, who treats the wound and places the sufferer in a glass-fronted cage heated to the appropriate temperature. As the effect of antibiotics on koalas is not yet precisely known, none are administered at this stage, either by injection or orally, for fear of destroying organisms present in the intestinal tract which are essential for the proper functioning of the animal's digestive system. The koala is checked continually, however, to detect the onset of severe shock or any other sign of deterioration, when desperate measures might have to be taken.

Severe shock does not occur, for two possible reasons. The subject has been handled before and also is very young. Another factor in the koala's favor is the promptness of his capture and transference to the dry, warmed cage at Taronga Park Zoo, for the cold winds of August are starting to blow, and late winter rains are sweeping the eastern coastal regions.

At Clareville and Avalon, by day, the sounds of voices and of traffic by water and by road are lost in the noise of the wind in the branches of the bangalay sheltering Talgara and her cub; by night, there are lights tossing in the darkness and glinting on white launches tugging at their lines.

The hour when Talgara finally decides to move on is the last before dawn, and nobody sees her go. Despite this, her absence is known by ten o'clock on the same morning, and, after the nearby trees have been searched without success, the disappearance of a koala and her cub from their usual places is reported to the Trust. Two disks —one for a full-grown koala and a smaller one for a cub— are pulled from a map on a wall and dropped, rather resignedly, into a cardboard box. There are now sixty disks on the map, whereas it is pretty certain there would be a hundred if the position of every koala in the district could be plotted. This estimate is thought to be conservative, as wildlife rangers maintain that the average person will detect no more than one koala in every three in open bushland—but of course the Barrenjoey peninsula is not exactly bushland. In any case, until a better method of counting is evolved, it is impossible to be quite sure whether the population of koalas in the area is increasing, diminishing, or holding steady.

So, for the time being, the members of the Trust and other similar bodies must continue their work by faith.

Nor is it light work, for it includes, among other things, the treatment of injured animals, the erection of signs informing the public that KOALAS CROSS HERE AT NIGHT, pleas to motorists and the owners of big dogs to have a care, and the distribution of suitable eucalypt seedlings to every resident who will plant one—or more, if possible.

Talgara keeps making her way slowly and erratically around the shores of Pittwater, sometimes through trees in gardens, sometimes through the less-built-over slopes of the ridges, but always getting closer to the broken terrain of the Ku-ring-gai Chase, a tract of country split by gullies and low sandstone cliffs supporting a great variety of bushes and stunted trees. Heathlands, some dry, some wet with seepage from the surrounding rocks, are not uncommon. By no stretch of the imagination could it be called an ideal habitat for koalas.

Shortly after starting out on her wandering excursion, Talgara attaches herself to a trio consisting of a male and two females. There are two months at least to go before the beginning of the mating season, and the male only once utters a call of any kind, a low grumbling cry when he detects the presence of another male somewhere in the darkness nearby. But neither is really interested in challenges, and so they go their ways.

After the wind drops, a cold, steady downpour overspreads the scene and, by excluding all detail, restores the distant view to what it must have been in similar weather by day a thousand years ago—gray ridges softened by the gray plumes of eucalypts, gray waters with gray cloud overhead and no evidence of any manmade thing. But by night, of course, there are the lights.

It is probably no more than a coincidence that a male koala and two females should have been in one another's company when Talgara caught up with them, for they now drift farther apart with each night's traveling. Both females, like Talgara, have dependent cubs, and Talgara and her own cub finally lose touch with the others when they stay awhile in a gray gum growing on a slope rising steeply out of the water. Some of the branches are level with a veranda, and a golden glow often reaches out to brighten the orange-pink color of some blotches on the tree's lizard-dark skin, now shining wet with rain.

The rain beats on the roof of the house and spatters the leaves around the koalas, to the faint accompaniment of orchestral music; and, just as incongruously, the odors of cooking flesh mingle with the scents of the eucalypts —and the uncomprehending Talgara might as well be back in her faraway gully for all the effect it has upon her.

As she changes her position in the tree, the cub sitting beside her springs onto her back and clings there high up near her neck, jockey fashion. Something sweeps silently overhead, hovers, then falls, and the life of a brushtailed possum in the next tree comes to an end as the talons of the huntress pierce his sides.

The owl beats up through the rain but descends again, as though her burden were too heavy, and alights rather nearer to the koalas. Limp in death, the possum hangs over the branch, a trickle of blood running from its mouth.

The koalas seem transfixed by the staring yellow eyes of the great bird of prey. When the wide wings lift, so also does Talgara raise a front paw, her own claws spread. But the owl flies swiftly down the slope of the hill, weaving between the trees, and disappears. The red marks on the fatal branch are already fading in the rain. A few moments later Talgara pulls down a spray of gray gum leaves, and her cub takes some for himself. Nothing has happened.

If the existence of koalas in the suburbs of a city seems extraordinary, then the presence of such a large nocturnal bird of prey as the powerful owl seems even more so, especially as its regular haunt is in heavy forest country. As such conditions no longer exist on the Barrenjoey peninsula, it is probable that the huntress came from some deep gully in the Ku-ring-gai Chase or in rugged scrub country farther west.

Cold southerly winds start to blow again in the last days of August, and Talgara stays in the vicinity of the gray gum. Her fur is almost always dark with rain, and when she is at rest her cub is usually in the warmest, driest spot available, huddled against her frontal fur under the roof of her bent head and shoulders.

# SEPTEMBER

For a while in the early part of September it is raining right down the eastern edge of Australia from Cape York in Queensland to Tasmania's South East Cape. In short, it is raining wherever there are koalas and in one place, Tasmania, where there are none.

Of the eucalypts in these regions, only the forest red gum covers the whole extent of koala country, though perhaps it does not quite reach to the southernmost point. It and the gray gum are probably the favorite food trees of the northern and middle groups of koalas; and the tallowwood is another in the top bracket of popularity, though its range is not as wide as that of the forest red gum.

Besides forest red gums, tallowwoods, and gray gums the middle latitudes of the Australian east coast have also

155

such eucalypts as the scribbly gums and the Sydney pepper-
mints, as well as a number of second-preference food trees
—Sydney blue gums, blackbutts, spotted gums, and others.

The favorite food of the koalas in Victoria seems to be
the manna gum, a tree that may flower for twelve months
of the year. This eucalypt grows as far north as parts of
Queensland but is nowhere else as fine as in the south.
In Victoria, too, are the messmates and the swamp gums;
and, sprinkled in various places from the extreme north to
the extreme south of the eastern side of the continent, in
various special habitats, are many other food trees, some
eucalypts, a few not—the bangalays and river red gums,
snappy gums and gray boxes, the swamp mahoganies and
some of the stringybarks, also the brush boxes and, when
there is nothing else available, the swamp turpentines and
the smooth-barked angophoras.

The wind and the rain which have now spread over
every part of this great tract of country are fiercest along
the central part of New South Wales. In the trees of the
Barrenjoey peninsula, at Port Macquarie—in the town
itself—and in the bush for a short distance inland, say,
at Gloucester as well as around Lismore and at Tweed
Heads, there is many a ball of drenched fur on high
branches, swirling in the gusts, or settled more stolidly at
lower levels as the koalas endure the storm.

In the coastal forests of Queensland and in the reserves
and sanctuaries of that state, the clouded air of this the
first month of spring is warm and humid in spite of the
rough weather, and the lightly furred koalas of the north,
though as wet as any others, do not have to overcome the

cold as do their shaggier, heavier kinsmen of Phillip Island and French Island on the southern coast of Victoria.

But the sharpest cold is over the Dividing Range, where sheep are dying in freezing conditions and the few koalas left on the plains cling to the eucalypts fringing some of the rivers. With no natural features to hinder them, the winds blow powerfully and steadily as winter goes out in a burst of fury.

Broken into fragments by the catastrophic changes that have swept away so much of its environment, the species would seem to be incapable of surviving anywhere except in the hitherto untouched coastal forests of Queensland. Yet where food trees grow, there koalas may be living— not many, perhaps, but some. Of course only a very small number of these possible havens is now inhabited, because once a local koala population is eliminated—by hunting or by the destruction of habitat, which may later partly regenerate—there is no channel of supply with any other community for the re-establishment of the group.

Wildlife rangers know that small clans of koalas are still being discovered in various places in eastern Australia and that not every discovery is reported, for fear that out-side interests, well-meaning and otherwise, may bring harm to the animals. So it would be foolish even to guess at the number of koalas living today, impossible to forecast their future. Though it is certain that their future, whatever it may be, will be decided by man, just as it is certain that the development taking place in the central and southern regions of eastern Australia today will be taking place in the forests of the north tomorrow. All in all, it would be difficult to find a more vivid illustration of the completeness of man's dominion over the wild creatures of this earth.

Koalas seldom try to conceal themselves, and the fact that one may curl up by day in the bushy top of a tall eucalypt and so be invisible from the ground is simply an accident. Probably it chanced to be feeding there when morning came. A koala is just as likely to sleep on a leafless branch in full view of every passer-by.

When koalas were plentiful, anyone with a rifle and a handful of cartridges could make pocket money in an hour or two, and this in spite of the fact that the skins, though well furred, are inferior to most others in over-all qualities and never brought a high price on the market.

That some millions of koalas have been shot is undisputed; that millions more were wiped out by the destruction of their habitat is also true. That is in the past. Besides, the destruction of some animal habitats must always take place—when it is necessary. But wholesale scorched-earth destruction is rarely, if ever, excusable.

All things considered, the ability of these specialized arboreal creatures to exist and also to increase in numbers wherever a sizable island of habitat remains is a miracle of contradiction—the very limitations of the animal serving in some cases to preserve it. However, most koalas so existing remain at risk because food trees growing along roadsides and in parks and reserves are not supported by enough plantings to offset natural losses, including those caused by the koala's habits of feeding on a favorite eucalypt until it dies from defoliation and of occasionally eating a seedling down to a stub.

Yet, in general terms, koalas seem able to live under conditions as they are at present at Avalon and Newport, Port Macquarie, Lismore, and one or two other places where the risk of being killed by dogs or automobiles has replaced the seasonal hazards of drought and bush fire in the wild. Otherwise, their only hope lies ultimately in the big reservation.

Koalas, more than most animals, keep inflexibly to their own way of life in the treetops and never covet the warmth and shelter to be had between the roofs and ceilings of human habitations. Their adherence to a leafy diet prevents them from being raiders of the garden, the orchard, and the garbage can, and their ability to exist without water limits their wants to one: food trees. Koalas make good neighbors because of their otherness.

When it comes to trying to assess the numbers of koalas in existence, however, there are difficulties without end, most of them springing from the facts that koalas do not use runways, do not require to visit streams or waterholes to drink, and cannot be enticed with food. As their distribution over wide tracts of forested country is often most uneven, it seems that the only way of making a survey is to sight every animal separately. Anyone who has tried to count the members of a small colony spread through the trees of a suburb will realize the impossibility of trying to carry out the same kind of work in wild bushland.

But, as it is known that koalas may be found today in

their natural surroundings in some of the forests of Queensland, as well as in a few colonies scattered southward down the east coast, the inquirer may hold fairly confidently to the opinion that the species is not under any immediate threat of extinction—though the populations of some of the colonies threaded through areas of human habitation are so minute that the risk of their being wiped out by epidemic is considerable. For instance, there are only about two hundred animals in and around Tucki Tucki, where Boorana is drying out after the rain.

Because of the many farms in the surrounding district, the amount of koala country is already limited to infrequent patches of woodland with some forest red gum, blackbutt, and two or three other kinds of eucalypt along the roadways; and a large proportion of the sapling eucalypts growing in places where they are safe from the clearing contractor's ax are now coming under threat from the ubiquitous camphor laurel.

Boorana is in a forest red gum standing by itself at the edge of an alluvial flat bounded on three sides by low hills. A creek flows into this amphitheater through a wide gap and, after describing a horseshoe-shaped course around it, goes out by the same gap but on the other side of it. Partly submerged trees and bushes mark the course the stream takes when it is running between its banks, but now the current is cutting straight across the entrance-and-exit gap and leaving the inundation of the flats a backwater.

It is more than a week since Boorana, under threat from a male traveling through the trees bordering the road on the ridge, fled to the forest red gum now surrounded by floodwaters. This is his eighth afternoon in the time-riven gum, which was a pretty poor specimen when he climbed it and is now a worse one. Some of its branches are dead, and Boorana has defoliated most of the others. If he can reach the few leaves remaining, he will undoubtedly do so and make certain the destruction of yet another of the food trees left in that locality.

Sunset's last pink reflection has faded from the calm floodwaters when the big male koala awakes and starts to groom the fur of his back with the joined combing claws of a hind foot, his leg pivoting with the readiness of the limbs of those toy animals that may be made to assume all kinds of amusing postures. As he scratches, he points his head skyward in a doglike attitude, at the same time plotting out the position of a rag of leaves. But he is in no hurry, and the stars are out when he bestirs himself sufficiently to start climbing. Without another upward glance, he selects the branch that will lead him to his objective, taking the second fork on the right and walking along the lateral until it becomes thin. When it bends so acutely that he must be head down if he goes on, he reaches out and tries to break off the end. He is soon successful in this, and when he has eaten the leaves he allows the broken branch to fall from his paws and hang there, swinging. By midnight he has snapped off seven more branchlets, so that only two eventually remain with leaves. He tries to break these also but fails. After descending to the lower part of the main trunk, he stops and scents the breeze. Then he launches unhesitatingly into the water.

The distance to the rise where ripples are lapping the grass tussocks is short, and he swims well. He emerges as lean as a kangaroo dog, shakes himself so vigorously that his ears slap loudly against his head, and makes for the nearest tree, a brush box, at a canter.

Some koalas often feed in brush box trees, but Boorana is not one of them. Nevertheless he is there, in the same tree, when the sun rises. Light and shadow bespeckle his fur, now quite dry again, and it would take a keen eye to detect him among the big leaves.

Solitary and timid though he may be, Boorana has now survived the shock of his enforced migration and his changed circumstances. Admittedly, he has declined from landholder to outcast, from a stout defender of territory to a creature living on the fringe of the community, but at least he is alive. And his bewilderment has passed. Perhaps it would be too much to say he has come to accept his changed status, or lack of status, and one may merely infer that any recollection he had of another kind of life has been blotted out by the experience of his present pillar-to-post existence—which now is, there being no past and no future. So he has nothing to be dazed about any longer. But he is moving gradually eastward, toward the coast, either by chance or by intent and, though intermittent and wavering, the trend continues.

Farther south, the tail end of the wet weather gives Sydney a farewell flick as it passes into the Pacific Ocean. Rain is spattering the glass front wall of an enclosure at Taronga Park Zoo where the young koala who was attacked by a dog is living in air-conditioned isolation—air-conditioned because wild animals under stress are particularly vulnerable to sudden changes of climate, isolation because when koalas decide to go they just go, and any other koala chancing to be in the way is simply climbed over, with the risk of having any injury made worse by the accident of a misplaced talon.

But for the treatment received from the head veterinarian at Taronga Park, there is no doubt that the victim would have died. The matted, bloodied fur on the patient's back would have quickly become saturated with rain if the koala had been left in a wild state, and cold winds would have done the rest. And if rain, wind, and shock had not killed him, septicemia almost certainly would have. As it is, he is released again into the tree from which he was taken, healed and definitely bigger and stronger from five weeks of feeding on the same varieties of eucalyptus leaves as are fed to the zoo's koalas in captivity, from five weeks of living in an equable temperature and having his food provided instead of being obliged to go and find it for himself.

Talgara has not moved far from where she was at the end of August. She and her offspring are in a gray gum, a very old tree and one of the tallest on a hillside of houses and tall trees. It is also an open tree, and its burden of foliage is light indeed, compared with its size. The tree's branches and its aerial strata of leafage cut the sky into inverted triangles with curved sides and a few other trifling irregularities. The koala in a fork near the end of a soaring branch is most conspicuous, and people have been stopping in the street and drawing the attention of other people to the koala way up there; a man asks a small boy how he would like to sleep like that on a thin and lofty perch that sways around from evening till morning, because that would be when the boy would be sleeping, at night and not in the daytime like a koala, and maybe, laddie, sometimes you could scrape a star or two off the sky. But the boy does not seem to hear. He just looks and wonders.

A freshening breeze is rustling the tree's arabesques of leaves. The weather is cool, and the breeze is making it cooler, so that soon there are only a few people watching. But the boy has not left. The sun is setting, but the light is clear and bright.

Then there are two koalas—the sleeper and a cub on the branch beside her. The boy cries out excitedly that the little koala was on the other's back all the time. He saw it there. He insists he saw it there.

The cub climbs to a fork about twice his own length above Talgara. Then he jumps, grabbing her around the neck and lurching sideways as both hind feet miss their mark. He scrambles to safety and waits awhile in his usual position on his parent's back. It was not a very impressive performance as far as agility is concerned.

The sky behind the gray gum is pink, and the plumes of the eucalypts on the western ridge are black when the cub again sets out, walking along the branch on this occasion and away from the larger koala, who so far has not stirred from her curled-up position. He wobbles when the branch swings, and finally sits down between two offshoots. Even then he teeters wildly, but it is clear he has a powerful grip with four sets of claws. Another, slenderer branch is beside the one he is on but somewhat below it. The distance must be about three times his own length, and it seems he is going to jump. He measures the leap and leans out, holding on with his hind feet, then changes his mind and clutches the branch with his forefeet, loses his balance, and swings to the underside to hang there upside down, sloth fashion. Though the watchers in the street are spellbound as the young koala wrestles his way back to the upper surface of the branch, there is in fact less danger in this fumbling maneuver than in any other separate incident of the series. Of course the realization of the onlookers that a fall from that height onto a paved surface would unquestionably be fatal does add a touch of the dramatic to the antics of a koala cub teaching himself to climb among great branches and to jump from one to another.

The cub prepares for a second attempt immediately upon regaining a normal position. Both branches are slim enough to be moving about in the breeze, but the next leap is bold and unhesitating, the landing a desperate affair, daring but clumsy, and saved from failure only by the strength of his legs. Actually, in this latest leap three sets of talons find an instant grip, and the frenzied grasping and struggling are caused by a hind foot clawing at the empty air as the youngster hauls himself up. He sits there quietly for a while, but he is not happy and starts to whimper as he shuffles backward down to the main trunk to ascend the rising lateral he has just left. Soon he is lying close in his parent's fur.

But in minutes he is on the move again. It is now nearly

dark, and even the sharp eyes of the boy can see him only vaguely as he climbs as far as the second fork and, following the thinner of the two prongs, creeps along until the inevitable happens and it abruptly dips, throwing the tiny adventurer into the terrifying head-down position. He starts to cry loudly. Whenever he tries to improve his grip, he slips a little farther and the branchlet dips a little more. His crying increases in volume and urgency until at last Talgara looks up. Unhurriedly she bestirs herself and follows him along the slim lateral for a certain distance, where she stops. She can do nothing except show anxiety, as she does. But to take another step would only worsen the situation, and she goes no nearer. The cub has now slipped to the leafy end of the branch. Here his hindquarters suddenly pivot toward the ground and leave him hanging by the forelegs but restored to a position where the hooks of his claws are again effective. His terrified squalling ceases as he drags himself higher, only to start again as the branch returns to its original shape, again putting him head down, though not seriously so. However, he sets up another whimpering cry and keeps it going until he has turned around and is backing down toward the main trunk.

Phlegmatic to the last, Talgara has returned to her former place and appears to be asleep when her cub arrives and settles down again on her back. She takes no notice of the several smacks on the head he delivers with his front paws, for he seems to hold her responsible for his recent predicament.

The koala youngling is fast approaching the age when

he will be able to survive independent of his mother and guardian. However, as the association between offspring and parent does not generally come to an end until the cub is somewhere between ten months and a year old, there is no reason why their present state of coexistence should not continue for a while.

The first month of spring goes out in brilliantly clear weather and a dry westerly wind, and the yellowtop ash in the Ku-ring-gai Chase is coming into bud.

# OCTOBER

In October a change comes over the behavior of the koalas at Tucki Tucki. The territories held by the males are more jealously guarded, and gone is the occasional casualness which sometimes allowed a newcomer like Boorana to live for a while unmolested as long as he did not trespass too blatantly on another's preserve. In its place everywhere is a growing belligerence.

Whenever two male koalas are within earshot of each other, even if neither is encroaching upon the other's boundaries, both will almost certainly keep on grumbling from time to time throughout the night. Though not frequent, these sounds show considerable variety—now a harsh grunting, then, perhaps an hour later, a gasping, strangled cry or a sudden explosive noise like a sneeze.

So far no mating has taken place, nor has there been

any vocal response from a female. At this preliminary stage of the breeding season it is threat and counterthreat until one koala retreats before the onslaught of a fiercer voice.

Though Boorana is not at present a target for any of these nocturnal challenges, he often hears them in the distance and is affected by them to the extent that he keeps wandering away from the danger zone. No other thing seems to trouble him. He crosses roads and paddocks as readily as though they were natural features of the original bush. Lights, human voices, and the noise of engines never meant much to him and now seem to mean less, though he does sometimes show signs of noticing them. He is always wary before jumping to the ground, but once completed a descent while a man was watching him from a distance of twenty paces. A deliberate movement, as of pursuit, caused the koala to quicken his pace as he was making for the next tree, but he slowed again and stopped to look down from the first branch.

Despite the differences around them, different sights, sounds, and smells, all the koalas in the district continue to live as though nothing has changed for a millennium, their only occupation the finding of food trees, with a brief side interest in the opposite sex each year during the mating season.

That spring on the north coast of New South Wales, like the one before it, brings no great change in the appearance of the countryside. There are no leafless trees to come into bud, other than the exotics planted in gardens and parks, and therefore there is no dramatic breaking of

the grip of a winter too easygoing to take a firm hold. But
the temperature rises from mild to warm, and, now that
the last of the winter rains has gone, the flow of migratory
birds returning from Siberia and the Arctic Circle is increasing.

Most days, and often through the nights, a koel is uttering the cry that has given it its second name of coo-ee
bird. Both the male in his purple-black plumage and the
brown-habited female quickly attract the attention of the
larger honeyeaters, friar birds, and wattle birds, which
harry them as though they realized the possibility of their
being chosen as foster parents for the young koel.

The visitors' strange calls are another new sound to
Boorana, most of the semi-migratory birds, including the
koels, having flown north before he was released at Tucki
Tucki. New or not, he pays no more attention to them
than he does to any of the other sounds around him,
though a male koel has been calling every night from a
silky oak close by. Boorana is feeding in a grove of blackbutt and spotted gum growing on a slope so steep that a
boulder dislodged from its bed would roll to the bottom
unless it collided with a tree trunk dead center. The other
side of the gully, too, is so precipitous and rocky that no
part of it could be used for grazing land.

Boorana has not gravitated to this remnant of original
bush because of any liking for spotted gum or blackbutt
but because here he has found peace. Sometimes the
lowing of cattle is audible from the paddocks surrounding
it, but usually there is only the rustle of the breeze. If he
wishes to cross to another tree he does so—as he is now

doing—and there is no other male to protest. He has
been feeding in a spotted gum and, having walked out
toward the end of one of its highest branches, is staring at
a blackbutt branch beneath him. Evidently he reckons
the distance too great to jump, for he backs down to the
main shaft. Competition has made most of the trees
straight and branchless right up to their crowns, and a
quick leap across an abyss so deep that only the pale trunks
of the flooded gums are discernible right down to the
forest floor will use up much less energy than a descent
to ground level followed by a climb back to the leaf canopy.

Of course exactly how much detail the koala can distinguish by the dim light of the stars cannot be known,
but the branch to which he transfers rises closer to the
outreaching limb of the blackbutt, although somewhat
above it. As he walks up the incline his nailless great toes
grip like thumbs. When he comes to his proposed take-
off point he swings to the underside of the branch and
settles back on his haunches. So he is now facing away
from the direction he intends to go, until he leans out
the length of a foreleg and, turning his head and shoulders,
measures the distance. His landing mark sways quietly
below him and about twice his own length to the side.
He continues to stare across the gap. He takes a little time
about it. Then he alters the grip of one of his hind feet,
twists his body some more, and lets go with his other
forepaw. If he were to change his mind now, his hind feet
could easily support him, but instead they launch him
powerfully into space, allowing such a wide margin for
error that he collides heavily with the other branch in-

stead of alighting upon it. Four sets of talons lock, and, graceful or not, he is safely across.

Both branches vibrate briefly, one from the thrust of take-off, the other from the shock of impact, and Boorana works his way, a thought restlessly, to the far side of the blackbutt, where he eats a few leaves before passing on to a tall brush box. He feeds there somewhat unhappily until dawn.

He spends the next night moving about the same group of trees, where the scent of the gland on his chest is now discernible. Suddenly he utters the cry of a holder of territory, but there is no response. Nor is there a response to his mating call, the simple fact being that no koala is near enough to hear it, and, as Boorana is out of the mainstream of community life in the locality, his only chance of attracting a mate is to intercept a newly matured female whose wanderings have taken her away from the older-established territories.

When this does eventually happen, however, the young female lured on by his calls discovers, on being more ardently courted, that she is not ready to mate after all, with the result that her tumultuous suitor finds himself pretty harshly dealt with every time he makes an approach. The punishment a female koala can inflict when she has the advantage of the higher position in a tree is considerable, and Boorana soon has a number of scratches on his head and neck as well as a slice out of his untagged ear.

The noise of these encounters brings a second male to the scene, and Boorana turns aside to meet the challenge. As a territory holder, he sounds as fierce as any other koala, but in this case threats are not enough, and the battle is joined on the trunk of a flooded gum. No worse site could have been chosen, and in moments the combatants plunge into the pad of decaying leaves on the ground, fly apart, and come together again like magnets, rolling over and over in a furious, grunting mass, struggling, scratching, and biting. And when the challenger turns to flee it is not over, for the defender again flings himself upon his enemy and, getting the crook of a muscular foreleg around his throat in a wrestler's stranglehold, starts to savage him about the side of the head. Though Boorana's incisors are not capable of inflicting a serious wound, their constant puncturing is enough to change the victim's cries to a squeal, which fades quickly to a choked wheezing and then into silence.

Boorana is back in the flooded gum within five minutes, and the loser, after lying as though dead, is stumbling downhill in defeat. If success does not soon attend him, he will be in danger of sinking into that state of inferiority from which his conqueror has now apparently emerged.

It is close to the end of October when Boorana mates with another female who chanced to stray within hearing range. She stays in his domain of second-class food trees for another forty-eight hours, then sets out across the paddocks for some tallowwoods in the bend of the road. The cold dew drenches her legs and flanks as she wades through the grass to the twanging, resonant cries of a pair of spur-winged plovers anxious about their nest among the tussocks. Though she sometimes glimpses their speeding shapes and hears their dangerous wings rip through the night air as they dive at her, she goes imperturbably on, and not even the destruction of the tallowwoods upsets her, for they have not yet been carted away and their leaves with the dew on them are still fresh.

Climbing through the wreckage, the female koala feeds as earnestly as though she had been starving, and when the sun rises she is asleep on a branch projecting from the heap. But she is not out of reach of the tallest man in the gang returning to finish the work started the night before. Her position is so ludicrously conspicuous that it causes much amusement. She is dropped into a chaff bag to be released later somewhere nearby.

Boorana would probably have remained in his new territory except for the thinning-out operation that takes place in an overpopulated area less than two kilometers away. Several young animals of both sexes are captured for transference to a forest of river red gums growing in a loop of the Murrumbidgee near the Riverina town of Narrandera in the south of New South Wales, and the opportunity is also taken to catch, check, and release any tagged koalas noticed, with the result that the community is so thoroughly disturbed that it scatters in consternation, some of its members wandering into the trees where Boorana is established. Three males are among the newcomers, and, after the usual interchange of threats, it is Boorana who retreats.

Of course in a week or so the invaders have returned whence they came, but by that time Boorana is some distance away, and with the effect of an even more alarming experience to work upon him. Soon after the catching and survey team left the district, a motorist noticed a koala with a red tag in his ear and made a report of the sighting. As the koala was then ten kilometers from the nearest place where tagging had been carried out it was immediately decided that the animal should be caught and inspected.

Accordingly, Boorana was captured that same afternoon by the ranger from Lismore, and the capture was surprisingly easy. Now free again, N.P.W.S. 86M appears to be no worse for his brief manhandling. He climbs freely and seems to settle down within minutes. The report says that his condition is only fair, and later comparison between his weight at that time and his weight when released at Tucki Tucki shows a slight loss.

Doubtless all recollection of the affair, as well as of the reason for his earlier flight, has vanished from his consciousness as swiftly as breath from a mirror, but a heightened nervousness remains, with some danger of development into that state of shock where the animal just suddenly gives up and, assuming the sleeping position, sinks rapidly into the lethargy that ends in death.

This does not happen, but Boorana is in retreat again and spends most of the night following his capture by the ranger in working along trees by the roadside, descending to the ground whenever he comes to a gap in the line and often passing a number of camphor laurels before climbing into a eucalypt for a short feeding session. By morning he has added another kilometer to the ten he has traveled from the reserve.

Boorana sleeps away a day in a forest red gum on top

of a ridge, where he is hidden from below by clusters of leaves which never cease to rustle in the warm easterly breeze. October is coming to an end, and a heat haze on the coastal plain is a film over the greenness of the grass and a forest of casuarinas. Threads of water shine from a swampy flat, and some streaks of smoke are drifting on parallel courses toward the hills.

The weather is as sunny but milder in Sydney. The strong westerlies of earlier spring have eased, and a light nor'easter is bringing the smell of burning from a brush fire on Barrenjoey. Talgara raises her head as the scent of it reaches her. Fire, even the faraway taint of it, always causes her concern, and she changes her position slightly in order to face directly into the breeze. Her cub is sitting on the branch above her. Though very much smaller than his parent, he has now acquired the true koala look, having lost the scrawny, elongated lines of the very young. Also, his fur is longer, and its fluffiness accentuates the round-ness of his face and head. The hair tufting about his ears is darker than his over-all grayness and gives him a quaint air of perkiness. Altogether, he must surely be one of the most fetching of young creatures, the more so because of his harmlessness, at present and in the future. The watcher knows that here is an animal that will live out its life without killing any other animal and without causing man any damage or inconvenience.

When it is dark, Talgara descends from her perch to visit a gray gum in the next garden. She often spends time in this tree, seeming to find its leaves particularly to her liking. Though her cub is ten and a half months old and could now fend for himself, he hurriedly backs down to the tree's main trunk and drops from there onto his parent's back. She has to steady herself as he bumps into place, but from there to the ground she has little difficulty in supporting his weight and makes no attempt to dislodge him. But he falls off of his own accord when she goes down a steep bank. Talgara walks steadily on, and the cub jumps up again and settles himself behind her shoulders, only to start slipping forward at once, finally to pitch over his mother's head exactly as before, both tumbles being the direct results of that weakness of the entire koala family, the inability to maintain an effective grip when in a head-down position.

The silhouette against the moon rising over Pittwater is of unusual shape as the two ascend the gray gum, but as soon as Talgara comes to a stop the cub slides down from her shoulders backward, walks along the branch, and pulls a spray of leaves for himself.

Mother and cub stay in the gray gum that night and sleep there next day. However, she is drifting gradually farther into the Ku-ring-gai Chase—not for any particular reason, for, unlike the old male koala on the ridge some hundreds of kilometers to the north, she is quite undisturbed, except perhaps by the approach of the breeding season. When she moves on, her cub goes with her, generally as a passenger, but not always. Sometimes she starts off without him and he has to hurry to catch up.

# NOVEMBER

It is early in the third month of spring; the hour is noon, and a heat haze is dancing on the sandstone ridges of the Ku-ring-gai Chase. Some of the kookaburras —and they abound in the Chase—have sought the deep bush and are drowsing there as though the sun's rays were striking down vertically instead of slantingly. But most of the other birds seem to be active enough, so perhaps it is the suddenness of the change to summery weather rather than the moderate height of the temperature, that has affected the big kingfishers.

The honeyeaters, small and large, are seldom at rest and seldom silent, and every now and then two or three of the liveliest and the noisiest, the wattlebirds, will swirl, quarreling, across a sage-green slope, all sparkling in the wind, then wheel as one and vanish into the trees. With their reckless swoopings and chasings and loud crackling cries, they are as inseparable from the Australian coastal bushland as old-man banksias, and rocks in summer too hot to touch, and cool-edged sea breezes.

Other calls and whistlings resound continually from every quarter, and many a twig projecting from the bushes of a swampy heathland between the ridges is capped again and again throughout the day by some dauntless holder of territory, often a yellow-winged honeyeater; and there is always one or more of them flickering and tumbling through the air in pursuit of an insect or diving into the sweltering humidity near the ground, where their nests are hidden amongst the bottlebrushes and spider flowers.

Because the heathlands are low-lying they are protected from the wind, which is whistling through the scrub on the ridges, where everything is moving—vibrating, fluttering, or waving—except the skeletons of last season's dwarf angophoras. Gray and many-pronged, they have stood the winter through as stark as dead thorn bushes. But lately new shoots have sprung from their bases, and some of their thicker branches, though apparently lifeless only a few short weeks ago, are loaded with buds. There are also, so mild is the weather, some clusters of pale yellow blossoms very like those of certain eucalypts, though more closely massed and therefore more spectacular, and any cluster not whipped by the wind is surrounded by a microcosmic universe of native bees and other winged insects. In wintertime the dwarf angophoras always look like forests that have died on the storm-swept cliffs of Lilliput, but they flower gloriously every summer. And their smooth-barked kinsmen, though they are as big as dwarfs are small, are strange trees too. They usually grow tall and straight in the deep gullies, but their Herculean limbs are always convoluted when they have room to spread; and their roots are able to flow like wax across great slabs of rock and fill up crevices and clefts or curtain down the sides of cliffs in their search for a way into the poor and sandy soil. When shadows play on the reddish trunks of the big angophoras with their patches of purple and silvery gray and blue, the bush sometimes seems to flame with bright, yet ghostly fire.

Just below the top of a ridge a long dark monolith is lying. It is as smooth as a whale's back, and waves of yellow-top ash are washing along its sides. Below this rock, clear down to the edge of an inlet, a multitude of trees is astir in the nor'easter; and on the spine of the ridge above the rock, in a scribbly gum, and in plain view from every direction, Talgara is asleep. She has been moving slowly along the peninsula for the last few days and is now deep into the Chase. Her cub is on the leeward side of her in another scribbly gum with a fairly dense head of foliage; and although no other kind of tree exists on the top of this exposed and arid eminence, there are the remains of some stranger from a kinder environment that clung long enough to life to leave behind a seamed and silvery trunk and the stub of a branch.

So rough is the terrain that, viewed from there, the Hawkesbury might be a cluster of lakes among fierce hills, instead of a confluence of drowned gullies and the outlet of a river to the sea. A wide-winged bird flying low across a bay, alternately flapping and gliding, comes suddenly into the force of the nor'easter and, towering effortlessly, expands into a sea eagle balancing in the gusts above the dead tree. He drifts closer in and waits awhile, watching. Only the vibration of his tail feathers tells of the strength of the wind pouring over the ridge. When his talons have closed around the branch he folds his pale wings and settles down in the sun. The dead tree is evidently a favorite perch, for the ground underneath is whitewashed with excreta. The eagle rouses only once, when the cub moves; but he does not see the motionless form of the full-grown koala and takes no further notice of the cub.

Three swamp wallabies emerge from the scrub onto the sun-drenched surface of the whale-shaped rock. The steady rushing of the wind, the restlessness of the bush around them, and the warmth of their sheltered position seem to lull them into a state of absolute quiescence.

A path leads up from the road to the rock. Far below, an automobile stops. Five people get out and start to climb. They are soon hidden by the roughnesses of the slope. The buck swamp wallaby rolls over on his back and stretches his head and neck luxuriously along the rock. His chest and belly fur is chrome orange. He and his two companions, both does, have come up to graze on the dry hillsides, which they frequent almost as much as they do the flatlands. It is the does who first hear the voices of the approaching party and give the alarm by bouncing lithely to their feet, but it is the buck who is first to glide with lowered head along a runway through the bush. A few minutes later the does melt into the shadows of the same escape tunnel. Last to leave is the eagle. Drifting into the air, he floats hesitatingly down the line of the slope like a huge butterfly looking for a place to alight but not finding it and always sailing on. He follows the water's edge and disappears behind the next headland.

After the climbing party has picked out various landmarks and discussed the oddness of a banksia cone, the ranger catches sight of the sleeping Talgara. But she is difficult to rouse, and the visitors have to be content with a partial awakening and a bemused stare from a half-opened eye. They say the koala is a "tame" one, and they will not be convinced otherwise, though the ranger reminds them that they are looking at an animal mainly nocturnal in habit and, further, one whose last few thousand years of existence as a species have left it with the impression that it is safe when in a tree—even a scribbly gum about twice the height of a man.

This explanation having been laughingly rejected, the visitors descend without noticing the cub at all, though he was almost within touching distance.

That night, when Talgara starts down the ridge, the cub goes with her, but now she takes no notice of him and he makes no real attempt to get closer to her. Yet he is quite definitely following and rests each day in the same tree or in a tree nearby.

There is a colony of twelve koalas in a sheltered gully where some gray gums and other eucalypts are growing, and where three mature males are becoming increasingly vocal each night as the breeding season progresses. Two of the females have already mated, and Talgara, as she

approaches the area, gives out a series of mewing responses
to the calling of a male. Crouching along a horizontal
branch, her suitor puts every ounce of his strength into
his uncouth roarings and coughings, until Talgara ceases
to answer and turns away to feed. But there is little doubt
that she will mate soon and that, having mated, she will
remain in this ancient forest. As for the cub, he will be
used to his present surroundings by the time he forgets to
hang about his mother, so he will probably stay also, until
he is old enough to incur the hostility of the holders of
territory. Because of the intervention of man, he is already
farther away from his sire than any koala could ever be
in normal circumstances. He is, in fact, some two hundred
kilometers south of the gully where he was conceived, and
Boorana is six hundred kilometers to the north of it.

The ground falls away steeply from the hilltop where
Boorana is curled in the fork of a tallowwood. Camou-
flaged by leaf shadows, he is not easy to see. He has been
there or thereabouts for a week or so, always moving into
another tree at night and always returning to the tallowwood to sleep by day.

Above the far ridges to the east the rumpled clouds,
flotillas of them, have been waiting since early morning.
Now, in the afternoon while the sun is still high, they
suddenly set sail and as they come closer they expand
until the last of the blue gaps between them vanishes and
the valley is plunged into a strange and unearthly twilight.
Thunder and lightning and furious gusts of wind proclaim
the breaking of the storm, and then, as though an Olym-

pian had shown annoyance at so much fuss, the whole magnificent display is bundled offstage in a torrential downpour and the sun shines out again, hotter than before.

Boorana sleeps on. His back has a bedraggled look, but the rest of him is dry. When the sounds of water trickling down the hillside cease, there is no sound at all. The leaves hang unstirring in the humid heat.

Badgered and chivvied by the holders of territory elsewhere, the koala might be expected to stay on in this untenanted place until his enormous appetite has defoliated the few eucalypts there. But the breeding season is approaching its peak, and the urge to seek out females is strong.

Awakening late in the afternoon, he stretches each leg in turn and starts to climb. Soon he is visible from below only when he leans from a dense plume of foliage to draw another bunch of leaves close enough to be touched with his muzzle; and half the time he does this, he immediately rejects the food he has won by allowing it to slip—regretfully, as it were—through a partly closed forepaw, which, with its long, hampering talons, is noticeably inferior in dexterity to the hands of his small relations the possums. He feeds in this selective manner until dusk, then, hesitantly and with many a wary glance over his shoulder, backs down to the tree's base and jumps to the ground. From there he sets out purposefully enough, even though his shorter hind legs do sometimes give the impression of hurrying to catch up. He stops at the edge of the grove and faces into a faint breeze welling out of the valley. Though he appears to be quite motionless, his head is actually swinging slightly and continuously from side to side and up and down, and he is so intent on scenting the air that his other faculties are temporarily eclipsed. Unfortunately, the smell of cattle grazing in the darkness nearby makes it difficult for him to distinguish other, subtler, odors, and so he goes on boldly down the hill.

He maintains a good pace for a while, but wading through thick grass is strenuous work and he tires suddenly. Lightly penciled across a starlit groundswell of paspalum, his trail now starts to twist and turn erratically, and his rate and mode of progress break down so markedly that he begins to look like an animal floundering in deep water. Nevertheless, he does arrive at a forest red gum.

Nor is this the only time Boorana has found a food tree in an area new to him. But whether those last minutes of casting about in a seemingly aimless manner were really no more than the final "homing in" on a target identified from a greater distance, or whether he did not realize that there was a food tree in the vicinity until he happened on it is something which cannot be deduced from the available facts, complicated as they are by the assumption that a koala's range of recognition would vary according to the power of the signal sent out—whether it emanated from a lone eucalypt or from a forest of eucalypts. Besides this, there are other forest red gums in the darkness some way up the valley from where Boorana, having fed, is now asleep.

Often between the hours of dusk and dawn he utters his mating call, but no answer comes back to him, and after two nights of plodding through pasturelands and having crossed roads and a canefield, he is checked by the Tuckean Swamp, which has been widened by rainstorms in the hills. Boorana follows the shoreline of floodwater until it is nearly light and then climbs into a swamp turpentine on the fringe of a casuarina thicket, where he sleeps for most of the day, waking in the afternoon to eat, rather unwillingly, of the tree's foliage. As soon as it is dark, he advances into marshy country, sometimes splashing across a shallow pool but generally keeping to the animal paths winding through the reeds. As always, he ignores the existence of the other creatures he encounters —the heron standing tall against the stars, the teal paddling watchfully away from him, and the egret that spreads its silvery wings and, ghostly in the dimness, rises into the air to seek a quieter fishing place.

At last only a single stretch of water separates him from higher ground. Reedbeds in capes and bays glisten faintly along the farther bank, and, though such an obstacle might well have caused many a larger animal to falter, the koala souses in with a flaring splash and starts swimming. He swims soundlessly with only part of his head showing, but a flight of black swans veers away and, beating over the trees, circles around and planes in for a second approach. White wingtips whip the air as the great birds brake before settling; then the commotion of splashdown smoothes away and the featherweight sounds of the night become audible again.

Sleek as an otter but not as deft, Boorana scrambles

through the reeds, shakes himself so energetically that the water sprays from him, and makes for a clump of straggly eucalypts.

The next day is heavily clouded, with repeated showers. Koalas do not usually move about much in the rain, but Boorana is restless. He wakes often and feeds intermittently until evening. Headlights and the rattling of a motor truck along a bush byway interrupt his descent, and he waits awhile before sliding the rest of the way down the tree trunk. Patches of stars are shining between the clouds, and the sky continues to clear as he moves uphill and later through a host of camphor laurel seedlings. Walking is easier when the stems of the camphor laurels become stouter and farther apart. The saplings beyond have grown into trees, and it is then that Boorana finds himself in another world. The whole nature of the camphor laurel forest is alien to him—the intense silence which begins just beyond the swishing of leaves under his feet, the unfamiliar resinous scents, and especially the absence of that sparkling interplay of light and shade which in clear weather lends such brilliance by night or day to the translucent heights of a forest of eucalypts.

Over the ridge's crest there is an expanse of open country studded with more camphor laurel seedlings, all relentlessly intent on farther widening the range of the species. But at least the going is unimpeded, and Boorana breaks into a lolloping canter. Having successfully squeezed between the slats of a dilapidated fence, he is confronted by a wilderness of overgrown paspalum where no cattle have grazed for many a month. Certainly he pauses—as well he may, when the length of his talons is remembered—but he shows no real resolution in his search for an alternative path and, characteristically, is soon plunging straight ahead. As he struggles to make headway, he often becomes entangled in the long, strong stalks of the paspalum, and each time this happens he is slower in regaining his feet, for, in common with many other wild creatures, he does not possess the reserves of strength necessary for protracted strenuous effort. To add to his distress, the seeds of the paspalum grass, most of them sticky with disease, are now massed so thickly around his eyes that he is unable to see properly, and he is near exhaustion when he emerges at the edge of the eucalypt forest near Uralba. Although there are now only dead, dry leaves and a few wisps of native grass under his feet, Boorana does not, cannot, go much farther, and in his ascent of the nearest tree—a bloodwood—he stops repeatedly to rest. Then, muddied as he is from the crossing of ditches and with his fur matted with paspalum seed, he makes an attempt to groom himself. But he is asleep before the work is fairly started.

Boorana is now rather more than twelve kilometers east of Tucki Tucki, where he was released some five months ago. Of course, if his incidental journeyings and his panicky flights from the threats of other males are counted, he has covered thrice that distance.

Next morning the sun rises out of a gray silk sea and shines across what was once a great paperbark swamp but is now a coastal plain checkered with the green of sugarcane and the brown of plowed earth. The pattern is most distinct, really, between the sand dunes bordering the beach and the Richmond River, which here flows roughly parallel with the shoreline. Between the river and the hills the land is undulating, with farms and pastures. On the Pacific Highway a yellow sports car is creeping north.

The only immigrant in years to have gained the forest near Uralba does not wake until the shadow of the hills, having spread beyond the highway and bedimmed the shining river, has reached the ocean's edge—an ocean whose deep, empurpled blue, though brilliant in the sun, contains already something of the mystery of night. Rather stiffly changing his position, the koala peers around and, by using the twin claws of whichever of his hind feet is the better able to deal with the part to be combed, applies himself until dark to the cleaning of his coat. Then he picks his way along the ridge to a gray gum—a tree which will retain the pitmarks of his talons until its bark is shed next season. But no evidence of his presence, including the rip-roaring love song he rasps out night after night, ever brings a challenge from any of the males established in a small and loose-knit community at the southern end of the forest. The newcomer moves slowly in that direction but stops when he arouses the hostility of another male. A vocal brawl quickly develops, with the holders of other territories joining in until everyone—there are not many—is raging against the interloper. Somewhat subdued by the clamor, but continuing to call, challenge, and call again, Boorana does not retreat, even if he does not advance, and on a night when the wind is blowing strongly he hears through the flutterings of innumerable leaves the mewing cry of a female. Her response is followed by a similar response from a second female, and Boorana starts back the way he has come.

The trio is out of earshot of the rest when his calling, often sinking to a low-pitched crooning, entices first one and then the other female to his tree. In spite of earlier blandishments and some interludes of soft invitation, the actual courting in both cases is as rampageous as ever, and in its penultimate stage, before actual copulation, the cacophony produced by the animals concerned bears no resemblance to the cries of any other species upon earth. After mating, none of the three seems to be aware of the presence of the others, though the females do tend to remain in the neighborhood of Boorana and the gray gum he has annexed.

By a combination of luck and an extra toughness of fiber that has enabled him to survive stresses and hardships that would have killed many another dispossessed landowner, Boorana now finds himself in a dry and fairly open eucalyptus forest that could fairly be described as the ideal habitat for his kind—and yet his situation is very like the one which obtained before he left the gully a full year ago. There is one vital difference, however; in the present instance he and the koalas around him are surrounded by so much bushland that their food supply should be assured for as long as the trees are allowed to stand. As they are in the middle of a farming district, the threat of the total destruction of the forest by an all-consuming wildfire is also remote, though there is always the chance of a partial burning by fires that might start inside the forest's boundaries.

It has been Boorana's good fortune, then, to have found a territory where the whipbird still sends out his startling call and the lyrebird has never learned to mimic the drone of the buzz-saw, and it now seems certain that the old koala—he is rising seven and past the middle line of middle age—will revert to the sedentary life of his kind as soon as the breeding season is over.

If, in the final analysis, his future remains in the hands of man, at least there is not much evidence here of man's existence—only the faraway noise of traffic on the Pacific Highway when the wind is in the right direction, and an occasional flash of sunlight from the fuselage of an aircraft flying overhead. But Boorana seldom raises his eyes to the skies, and the distant thunder of engines is to him nothing.

CONVERSION TABLE

GLOSSARY

BIBLIOGRAPHY

INDEX

# CONVERSION TABLE

| METRIC | | U.S. EQUIVALENT |
|--------|---|-----------------|
| | LENGTH | |
| centimeter | | 0.3937 inch |
| meter | | 3.2808 feet |
| | | 1.0936 yard |
| kilometer | | 0.6214 mile |
| | WEIGHT | |
| kilogram | | 2.2046 pounds |

# GLOSSARY

ANGOPHORA (*Angophora costata*). The smooth-barked angophora, smooth-barked apple, rusty gum, or red gum. A large tree with massive branches and thin foliage.

ANGOPHORA, DWARF (*Angophora cordifolia*). See Apple, dwarf.

ANGOPHORA, SMOOTH-BARKED. See Angophora (*A. costata*).

APPLE, DWARF (*Angophora cordifolia*). Shrub, or very small tree, of the dry ridges of Hawkesbury sandstone.

APPLE, SMOOTH-BARKED. See Angophora (*A. costata*).

ASH, YELLOWTOP (*Eucalyptus luehmanniana*). One of the mallees. A small sapling-sized tree common on the sandstone ridges around the Sydney area.

BANGALAY (*Eucalyptus botryoides*). A medium-sized eucalypt and a koala food tree. Preferred habitat, good soil near the edges of the sea and its inlets.

BANKSIA (*Banksia serrata*). "Old-man banksia." Small to medium-sized trees, often gnarled and stunted. There is a variety of banksias from *serrata* down to bushes.

BLACKBUTT (*Eucalyptus pilularis*). Large forest tree with dark, fibrous bark on bole and smooth, pale upper limbs. Koalas occasionally eat its foliage.

BLOODWOOD (*Eucalyptus gummifera*). Grows to a fair height when in deep soil. Sometimes exudes a red gum, or kino. Foliage sometimes eaten by koalas.

BOTTLEBRUSH. See Callistemons.

BOX, BRUSH (*Tristania conferta*). Rain-forest tree, now spreading to other habitats. Leaves sometimes eaten by koalas.

BOX, GRAY (*Eucalyptus moluccana*). Rough-barked eucalypt with wide head of foliage.

BUTCHER BIRD (*Cracticus torquatus*). The gray butcher bird. Swift flier. Lives on insects, small birds, lizards, and mice.

CALLISTEMONS. Bottlebrushes. Several species of shrubs and small trees.

Flowers have bristle-like stamens and the over-all shape of bottle-brushes.

CAMPHOR LAUREL (*Cinnamomum camphora*). Though a beautiful tree in its own right, the introduced camphor laurel is so well suited to parts of the Australian continent, especially the north coast of New South Wales, and its seeds are being spread by so many of the native birds, that it has become the predominating tree of some suburban and rural scenes, overwhelming the native flora. It is still spreading, and at an accelerating rate.

CASUARINA. A group of trees including the swamp oak, she-oak, forest oak, and bull oak. They bear some resemblance to pine trees with very long "needles," but are not related.

CICADA. Group of large sapsucking insects that make a loud drumming noise, especially in very hot weather.

CROW (*Corvus cecilœ*). In the field the crow is indistinguishable from the raven. Both birds are omnivorous.

CURRAWONG (*Strepera graculina*). The pied currawong, large black-and-white birds. Food: insects, berries, seeds, fruit, and small animals.

DINGO (*Canis antarcticus*). The warrigal, or Australian wild dog.

DOG, CATTLE. Strong, active dingo cross for droving. A silent, tireless worker.

DOG, KANGAROO. Dog used for hunting kangaroos. Generally a greyhound or greyhound cross.

EAGLE OWL. *See* Owl, powerful.

EAGLE, SEA (*Haliæetus leucogaster*). The white-breasted sea eagle.

EAGLE, WEDGE-TAILED (*Aquila audax*). Largest of the Australian eagles and one of the largest in the world.

ECHIDNA (*Tachyglossus aculeatus*). The spiny anteater or "native Porcupine." The echidna and the platypus are the only egg-laying mammals. A "rolled-up" echidna resembles a grass tussock that has been singed by fire and is starting to send out new shoots.

EGRET, WHITE (*Egretta alba*). Also known as great egret and white crane.

ERIOSTEMON. Native flowering shrubs.

FOX (*Vulpes vulpes*). The European fox, now widespread in Australia.

FRIAR BIRD (*Philemon corniculatus*). Noisy friar bird. Nomadic, one of the larger honeyeaters. Pugnacious. Has black head without any feathers.

FROGMOUTH, TAWNY (*Podargus strigoides*). Grayish, soft-plumaged nocturnal bird. Fairly common.

GLIDER (*Schoinobates volans*). The greater glider, a marsupial. Eats mainly the leaves and blossoms of certain ecualypts.

GLIDER, SUGAR (*Petaurus breviceps*). A small gliding possum. Food: insects, fruits, blossoms.

GRASS, PASPALUM (*Paspalum dilatatum*). Introduced grass from South America. Excellent feed for dairy stock.

GRASS TREE (*genus: Xanthorrhoea*). Also called "blackboy" because fire-blackened trunk and tall flower spike resemble an aborigine carrying a spear.

GUM, FLOODED (*Eucalyptus grandis*). Eucalypt with smooth, straight trunk generally free of branches for up to three-quarters of its length. Grows to 55 meters.

GUM, FOREST RED (*Eucalyptus tereticornis*). Old trees grow to great size. A favorite koala food tree.

GUM, GRAY (*Eucalyptus punctata*). Large eucalypt of open habit, with gray bark not unlike a lizard's skin. Favored koala food tree.

GUM, MANNA (*Eucalyptus viminalis*). One of the main food trees of koalas in the southern part of their range, where it often grows to a great height.

GUM, RED. *See* Angophora (*A. costata*).

GUM, RIVER RED (*Eucalyptus camaldulensis*). Sturdy, spreading tree of the river banks and the flood plains. Carries a good head of foliage for a eucalypt. Favorite koala food tree.

GUM, RUSTY. *See* Angophora (*A. costata*).

GUM, SCRIBBLY (*Eucalyptus hæmastoma*). Tough little eucalypt of the rocky ridges. Good koala food tree.

GUM, SNAPPY (*Eucalyptus racemosa*). Very like the scribbly gum (*E. hæmastoma*) but taller and of better shape. Some say it is a scribbly gum in good circumstances.

GUM, SPOTTED (*Eucalyptus maculata*). Tall, straight eucalypt generally growing in pure stands. Pale trunk often retains small patches of bark for a while after the rest is shed. Koalas sometimes eat sparingly of its foliage.

GUM, SWAMP (*Eucalyptus ovata*). Grows in the cooler southern parts of the east coast region of Australia. Medium-sized and sometimes stunted, according to the nature of the soil. Likes moist situation.

GUM, SYDNEY BLUE (*Eucalyptus saligna*). Tall (50 meters), smooth-shafted tree. Bark has blue tinge.

HERON (*Ardea novæ-hollandiæ*). White-fronted or white-faced heron. Sometimes called a "blue crane."

HONEYEATERS. There is a very large number of these nectar- and insect-eating birds in Australia.

HONEYEATER, YELLOW-WINGED (*Meliornis n-ovæ-hollandiæ*). One of the smaller honeyeaters. Also known as New Holland or white-bearded honeyeater.

IRONBARK. A group of eucalypts with very hard black and dark gray bark arranged in vertical deep-raked, flat-topped ridges.

KOEL (*Eudynamys orientalis*). A cuckoo, the coo-ee bird. Often heard, but seldom seen. Its strange call is sometimes repeated at intervals of a few seconds for long periods, especially at night.

KOOKABURRA (*Dacelo gigas*). The giant kingfisher; also the laughing kingfisher, laughing jackass, and settler's clock.

LANTANA (*Lantana camara*). Introduced bush with small bright flowers. Has spread over considerable areas of farmland and has also invaded the native bushland.

LORIKEET, RAINBOW (*Trichoglossus moluccanus*). Small parrot—noisy, numerous, and brightly colored.

LYREBIRD (*Menura superba*). The famous mimic. Large bird of the forest floors, deep gullies, and banks of streams—provided there is dense cover. The male's tail, when spread in display, is shaped like a lyre.

MAGPIE (*Gymnorhina tibicen*). Active, pugnacious bird. Black-and-white markings. Beautiful flutelike notes.

MAHOGANY, SWAMP (*Eucalyptus robusta*). Favored koala food tree, medium-sized with rough, fibrous bark and leaves of a deeper green than those of most other eucalypts.

MELALEUCA. The paperbarks. Their bark may be stripped off in thin, papery sheets. The group contains shrubs and small "rounded" trees.

MESSMATE (*Eucalyptus obliqua*). Rough-barked eucalypt which grows to a great height.

MINER, NOISY (*Myzantha melanocephala*). A honeyeater. The soldier bird or garrulous honeyeater.

MOTH OWL (*Aegotheles cristata*). The owlet nightjar, fairy owl, goatsucker. Small, insectivorous nocturnal bird.

MOUSE, MARSUPIAL. Australia contains a variety of these small mammals.

MUSKS (*Glossopitta concinna*). Very small lorikeet. Nomadic, it follows the blossoming of the eucalypts.

OTTERS. There are, of course, no otters in Australia.

OWL, BOOBOOK (*Ninox boobook*). A small owl. Food: insects, mice.

OWL, POWERFUL (*Ninox strenua*). The largest nocturnal Australian bird of prey.

PAPERBARKS. *See* Melaleuca.

PEPPERMINT, SYDNEY (*Eucalyptus piperita*). Big, heavy-limbed tree of open growth. Small branches are smooth; trunk and larger branches are covered with rough bark. A koala food tree.

PHEASANT, SWAMP (*Centropus phasianinus*). The pheasant coucal or coucal. Large cuckoo frequenting the heavy growth of grass and bush around creeks and swamps. Builds it own nest and rears its young. Strange call is often written as *coop, coop*.

PINE. Introduced tree sometimes planted as windbreak.

PLOVER, GOLDEN (*Pluvialis dominica*). Migratory wading bird arriving in Australia in September/October and returning north in March or April.

PLOVER, SPUR-WINGED (*Lobibyx novæ-hollandiæ*). One of the largest of the plovers. Non-migratory. Has a spur on each shoulder. Loud, ringing call.

POSSUM, BRUSH-TAILED (*Trichosurus vulpecula*). The common possum. Omnivorous. Strong, active marsupial with amazing climbing ability.

POSSUM, GLIDING. *See* Glider.

POSSUM, PYGMY (*Cercartetus nanus*). Nocturnal mouse-sized marsupial possum. Lives on insects, nectar, blossoms.

PRIVET (*Ligustrum sp.*). Introduced, strong-growing plants which may reach the size of a tree. They seed and flower profusely and have spread widely, especially in good soil in gullies and along watercourses, overwhelming the native bushes and seedlings.

RAVEN (*Corvus coronoides*). Bird of the crow family. Omnivorous.

ROSELLA, CRIMSON (*Platycerus elegans*). Brightly colored parrot.

SANDERLING (*Crocethia alba*). A wading bird arriving in Australia from the Arctic in September and leaving in April.

SCALY-BREASTED GREEN-AND-GOLD (*Trichoglossus chlorolepidotus*). The scaly-breasted lorikeet. Smaller than the rainbow (*Trichoglossus moluccanus*), but larger than the musk (*Glossopitta concinna*) lorikeets. Fine yellow edging to green breast feathers gives fish-scale effect.

SEA CURLEW (*Numenius madagascariensis*). The eastern curlew. A migrant, arriving in Australia in the southern spring and returning north in April to nest in Siberia.

SILKY OAK (*Grevillea robusta*). Stout tree with straight trunk and fernlike leaves. Spectacular light orange-yellow blossoms.

SPIDER FLOWER (*Grevillea buxifolia*). The gray spider flower. This flower, which grows on a small bush plentiful in the sandstone country, bears some resemblance to a large, leggy spider.

STRINGYBARKS. A small group of eucalypts with stringy bark, usually furrowed, which may be stripped off by hand in long fibrous ribbons.

SWAN, BLACK (*Cygnus atratus*). Australia's only swan. Black, with scarlet bill. The white ends of the wings flash brilliantly when the bird is in flight.

TALLOWWOOD (*Eucalyptus microcorys*). A fine eucalypt, tall and widespreading. Koala food tree.

TEAL, CHESTNUT (*Anas castanea*). Brightly colored species of small wild duck.

TURPENTINE (*Syncarpia glomulifera*). Tall and shapely tree with a fine head of deep green foliage.

TURPENTINE, SWAMP (*Tristania sauveolens*). Medium-sized tree, not unlike a small specimen of the turpentine *Syncarpia glomulifera.*

WALLABY. One of the smaller specimens of the kangaroo family.

WALLABY, SWAMP (*Wallabia bicolor*). Also the black-tailed swamp wallaby. A sturdy wallaby of the thick scrub, swamp margins, and dry ridges.

WATTLE. The acacia. Often the first plants to re-establish themselves on cleared land, the wattles range in size from bushes to small trees. Many of them produce yellow or golden puffball blossoms in great profusion.

WATTLE BIRD (*Anthochæra carunculata*). The red wattle bird is one of the larger honeyeaters. It is noisy, active, and pugnacious.

WEDGETAIL. *See* Eagle, wedge-tailed.

WHIMBREL (*Numenius phæopus*). Wading bird migrating to Australia in September or October and returning north in March/April.

WHIPBIRD (*Psophodes olivaceus*). Also the coachwhip bird. A bird of the undergrowth and ferny places. It is about the size of a thrush, and its call is a long note, ending in a sound like the crack of a whip.

WOMBAT (*Vombatus hirsutus*). The common wombat. A heavily built burrowing marsupial. A herbivore. Nocturnal.

# BIBLIOGRAPHY

Barclay-Rose, Antony. "Analysis of Gut Content of Currawong and White-headed Pigeon," in *Birds* (Sydney), Vol. 5, No. 6 (1971).
———. "Food of Some Australian Birds," in *The Emu* (Melbourne), Vol. 73, Part 4, 1973, pp. 177–183.
———. "Notes on the Powerful Owl," in *Birds* (Syndey), Vol. 5, No. 6, 1971.
Child, John. *Trees of the Sydney Region.* Melbourne: Cheshire-Landsdowne, 1968.
Cockram, Frank A., and Jackson, A.R.B. "Isolation of a Chlamydia from Cases of Keratoconjunctivitis in Koalas," letter in *Australian Veterinary Journal*, Vol. 50 (February 1974).
Dickens, Russell K., M.V.Sc. *The Haematology of the Koala (Phascolarctos cinereus. Goldfuss. 1817).* Sydney: Sydney University, 1974 M.V.S. thesis).
Eberhard, Ian H., McNamara, John, Pearse, Rodney J., and Southwell, Ian. "The Ingestion and Excretion of *E. punctata* and Its Essential Oil by the Koala," *Australian Zoological Journal* (Sydney), 1975.
Fleay, David. *Gliders of the Gum Trees.* Melbourne: Bread and Cheese Club, 1947.
Hindwood, Keith A., and Hoskin, Ernest S. "The Waders of Sydney," in *The Emu* (Melbourne), Vol. 54, Part 4 (1954), pp. 217–255.
Millett, Mervyn. *Australian Eucalypts.* Melbourne: Landsdowne Press, 1969.
Pratt, Ambrose. *The Call of the Koala.* Melbourne: Robertson and Mullens, 1937.
Ride, W.D.L. *A Guide to the Native Mammals of Australia.* Melbourne: Oxford University Press, 1970.
Troughton, Ellis. *Furred Animals of Australia.* Sydney: Angus and Robertson, 1941.

# INDEX